**Editor**
Kim Fields

**Consultant**
Barbara Forslund Cracchiolo,
O.T.R.

**Editorial Project Manager**
Mara Ellen Guckian

**Editor-in-Chief**
Sharon Coan, M.S. Ed.

**Illustrators**
Bruce Hedges
Rene Christine Yates

**Cover Artist**
Brenda DiAntonis

**Art Coordinator**
Kevin Barnes

**Art Director**
CJae Froshay

**Imaging**
Ralph Olmedo, Jr.
Temo Parra

**Product Manager**
Phil Garcia

**Publishers**
Rachelle Cracchiolo, M.S. Ed.
Mary Dupuy Smith, M.S. Ed.

# ACTIVITIES FOR Gross Motor Skills DEVELOPMENT

**Written and Compiled by**
Jodene Lynn Smith, M.A.

***Teacher Created Materials, Inc.***
6421 Industry Way
Westminster, CA 92683
www.teachercreated.com

**ISBN-0-7439-3690-6**

©*2003 Teacher Created Materials, Inc.*

Made in U.S.A.

The classroom teacher may reproduce copies of materials in this book for classroom use only.
The reproduction of any part for an entire school or school system is strictly prohibited. No part
of this publication may be transmitted, stored, or recorded in any form without written
permission from the publisher.

# Table of Contents

# Introduction

The term "busy bees" is particularly appropriate when describing young children. Children from ages 2–5 are on the go much of the time. Their interest in exploring and learning new things is exciting to watch. However, reports about the skill and activity levels of older children are very disturbing and, as educators, demand our attention. With the loss of many physical education specialists, instruction and monitoring of a child's motor skills is being required of the classroom teacher. This book has been designed to help the classroom teacher with this prospect. The entire purpose of this book is to provide practical and easy ways teachers can help students develop gross motor skills while increasing their activity level.

Provided in the introductory pages of *Activities for Gross Motor Skills Development* is background information on motor planning, body awareness, bilateral integration, and tactile awareness. An understanding of the basics of each of these areas will help teachers in monitoring and instructing students in motor skills. Included is information on each topic, characteristics of children having difficulty within each area, and suggestions for helping these students. Included at the end of the introduction are developmental checklists of gross motor skills of children from ages 18 months to 60 months (1½ years to 5 years).

Following the introductory pages, the book is divided into seven major sections. "Spatial and Body Awareness" contains activities that help each student understand his or her own body's potential for movement. Through action songs and poems, as well as creative movement activities such as using streamers, the student will develop a better understanding of his or her own personal space and the space around him or her.

Activities devoted to walking, running, jumping, and more are included in the section, "Locomotor Skills." Developing these skills is crucial to helping students gain further success in any other movement experience. The "Ball Skills" section provides ideas for learning to throw, catch, and play with balls.

If you have equipment available at your site, the "Equipment" section of the book will be of interest to you. Provided are activities and ideas for major pieces of equipment which most schools have available, including: playground equipment, hula hoops, jump ropes, parachutes, and more.

An essential part of early childhood education is providing activities which require students to use all of their senses. A whole section of the book has been devoted to "Sensory Tables." Included are ideas for types of sensory tables, as wells as ways to adapt and change sensory tables in order to maintain student interest.

The section titled "Creative Play" contains ways to stimulate play through painting, collections of materials, music, cooking, and much more. Finally, "Games, Obstacles, and Relays" contains rules for games and ideas for obstacle courses and relay races which require students to incorporate many gross motor skills in order to complete them.

In each section, brief activity descriptions and illustrations help the teacher understand the activities easily. A materials list, for organizational purposes, helps the teacher easily determine whether the equipment needed for the activity is available. Oftentimes, a rule of the game or the format in which an activity takes place can be changed slightly to work with other pieces of available equipment.

Teachers will enjoy the variety of activities found in this book. Students, even the most reluctant, should enjoy participating in the activities. Above all, the classroom teacher will feel more confident in providing activities that will help students develop gross motor skills, as well as be more active.

# Body Awareness

*Body awareness* refers to the student's ability to know where his or her body is in space. Opening jar lids without looking at your hands, gauging how far to duck your head when getting under a low table, and sitting down without constantly looking at the chair all require you to have a good sense of where your body is in space.

Other indicators of a student's sense of body awareness include how close or far away he or she sits from other students and how hard or how gently items are pulled apart or put together. Students who have poor body awareness appear clumsy, walk by shuffling their feet on the floor, have difficulty climbing on playground equipment, and continually bump into other students.

Heaving, lifting, pushing, pulling, and carrying all help your brain to know where your body is located in space. Suggestions for helping students who are having difficulty with body awareness are listed below:

- Carry a heavy stack of books.
- Do frog jumps.
- Do jumping activities.
- Do push-ups and pull-ups.
- Play on a jungle gym. Start on low equipment and then advance to taller equipment.
- Play on the monkey bars.
- Play Simon Says.
- Play tug-of-war.
- Push feet and/or hands against the walls as if to push the walls out.
- Swing by lying on the stomach rather than sitting on the swing seat.
- Take out the garbage.
- Try beanbag activities.
- Use teeter-totters.

A student who is having difficulty with body awareness may exhibit one or more of the following characteristics or behaviors:

- ○ Student appears clumsy.
- ○ Student appears disorganized with personal belongings.
- ○ Student falls out of a chair.
- ○ Student frequently breaks things.
- ○ Student has difficulty moving without looking at his or her arms and legs.
- ○ Student has difficulty putting on his or her jacket, sweater, or backpack.
- ○ Student has difficulty standing in line.
- ○ Student has poorly developed fine motor skills.
- ○ Student is unable to climb on playground equipment.
- ○ Student pushes too hard or too softly on a pencil or crayon.
- ○ Student rips the paper when erasing.
- ○ Student shuffles feet when walking.

# Motor Planning

P9-ELV-804

*Motor planning* refers to a student's ability to figure out how to do a new motor task. Some of our motor actions are routine, such as bringing a spoon up to the mouth to eat. If we are asked to bring the spoon to a knee or up to an ear, we would have to think about the movement and plan the motor action. That is motor planning. Prior to any movements, the brain has to organize all the environmental information so that the body will move in the direction needed with the appropriate speed, force, and timing. The ability to motor plan depends on thinking skills as well as sensory motor development.

Below are some suggestions for helping students who are having difficulty with motor planning:

- Break tasks down into smaller steps.
- Do a lot of rolling, jumping, and ball activities.
- Give one direction at a time.
- Guide students through the motor action.
- Have a check-off sheet for each student to check off each step as he or she completes the task.
- Have students orally repeat directions.
- Keep verbal directions to a minimum.
- Minimize oral and auditory distractions in the room.
- Play games with movement and rhythm.
- Play imitation games, such as "Simon Says" or "Follow the Leader."
- Use visual cues.

A student having difficulty with motor planning may exhibit the following characteristics or behaviors:

- ○ Student appears clumsy.
- ○ Student appears messy.
- ○ Student has an awkward grip on a pencil or crayon.
- ○ Student has difficulty running, jumping, and dancing.
- ○ Student has trouble finishing a task on time.
- ○ Student imitates the actions of other students, rather than figuring out movements for himself or herself.
- ○ Student is unable to follow directions when directed to perform an unfamiliar task.
- ○ Student is unable to sequence motor actions required for a new skill.
- ○ Student may resist, act out, or refuse to do an activity.
- ○ Student takes a long time learning a new skill.
- ○ Student watches others so he or she can figure out how to do a motor action.
- ○ Student will not attempt new motor actions.

# Bilateral Integration and Crossing the Midline

*Bilateral integration* refers to the student's ability to use both sides of his or her body during an activity. Sometimes our hands are doing the same movement, and at other times they are acting separately. When catching a ball, both hands are performing the same motion. When coloring or writing, one hand is doing the movement while the other hand is holding the paper.

*Crossing the midline* refers to the student's ability to cross over the midline of the body. (The midline is an imaginary line that runs through the body cutting it in half from head to toe.) Crossing the midline is the student's ability to reach with the right hand or right leg over the midline to the left side of the body. Crossing the midline means moving an arm or leg, not moving the body, and twisting toward one side.

Activities that necessitate using both hands, both feet, or crossing over the midline help develop the neuron pathways within the brain for reading, writing, and mathematics. Coordinating both sides of the body is needed for the development of many gross and fine motor skills.

Below are some suggestions for helping students who are having difficulty with bilateral integration and/or crossing the midline. See pages 8–10 for additional activities.

- Carry heavy objects using two hands.
- Do jumping jacks.
- Do mixing bowl activities—stir, pour, and measure.
- Jump rope.
- Play basketball.
- Play clapping games and use rhythm sticks.
- Play musical instruments.
- Play two-square or four-square.
- Practice cutting.
- Practice jumping with feet apart and landing with feet apart.
- Practice opening snack and lunch containers.
- Ride a bike.
- Roll clay.
- Scissor-walk on a line.
- Sharpen pencils using a manual pencil sharpener.
- Skip.
- String beads.
- Swim.
- Tear paper.
- Tie shoes or tie yarn bows on packages.
- Turn a hand egg beater.
- Use pop beads or interlocking blocks.
- Wind wind-up toys.

# Bilateral Integration
# and Crossing the Midline *(cont.)*

A student who is having difficulty with bilateral integration and/or crossing the midline may exhibit one or more of the following behaviors or characteristics:

○ Student turns his or her body to avoid crossing the midline.

○ While writing or coloring, the student moves his or her whole body when going across the paper, rather than just moving his or her arm.

○ Student does not hold the paper down with one hand while using the other hand for writing.

○ Student switches hands during a fine motor task. He or she uses the right hand for reaching and putting items on the right side of his or her body, and uses the left hand for reaching and putting items on the left side of his or her body.

○ Student switches his or her hands for writing or coloring when coming to the midline of the body; he or she writes with the left hand on the left side of the paper, and then switches at the midline to the right hand.

# Bilateral Integration and Crossing the Midline *(cont.)*

Finger plays that require students to use both hands are an excellent way to develop bilateral integration, and allow students to practice crossing the midline.

**Note:** The traditional finger plays included in this book are from the oral tradition and cannot be attributed to a specific author.

### Itsy, Bitsy Spider

The itsy, bitsy spider went up the water spout.
*(Use first two fingers of one hand to walk up the other arm.)*

Down came the rain and washed the spider out.
*(Flutter fingers down.)*

Out came the sun and dried up all the rain.
*(Make circle over head with your arms.)*

And the itsy, bitsy spider went up the spout again.
*(Use first two fingers to walk up the other arm.)*

### Baby Bumblebee

I'm bringing home a baby bumblebee.
*(Cup one hand over the palm of other hand.)*

Won't my mommy be so proud of me?
*(Move hands up and down, holding hands as above.)*

I'm bringing home a baby bumblebee.
*(Continue the action above.)*

OUCH! He bit me!
*(Open up hands.)*

# Bilateral Integration and Crossing the Midline (cont.)

## This Old Man

This old man, he played one,
*(Hold up one finger.)*
He played knick-knack on his thumb.
*(Tap thumbs together.)*
*Chorus:*
With a knick-knack, paddy-whack, give a dog a bone,
*(Make right hand into fist, point thumb over shoulder.)*
This old man came rolling home.
*(Roll your hands, one over the other.)*
*(Continue, substituting the following lines as you count to ten.)*
This old man, he played two,
*(Hold up two fingers.)*
He played knick-knack on his shoe.
*(Tap on shoe with fingers.)*
This old man, he played three,
*(Hold up three fingers.)*
He played knick-knack on his knee.
*(Tap on knee with fingers.)*
This old man, he played four,
*(Hold up four fingers.)*
He played knick-knack on the door.
*(Use fist to pretend to knock on a door.)*
This old man, he played five,
*(Hold up five fingers.)*
He played knick-knack on his hive.
*(Make a fist with one hand. Use the index finger of the other hand to tap on the fist.)*
This old man, he played six,
*(Hold up six fingers.)*
He played knick-knack on his sticks.
*(Tap index fingers together.)*
This old man, he played seven,
*(Hold up seven fingers.)*
He played knick-knack up to heaven.
*(Use index finger to point to the sky.)*
This old man, he played eight,
*(Hold up eight fingers.)*
He played knick-knack on his plate.
*(Make a circle with one arm by touching the hand to the stomach and holding the elbow out. Use the index finger to tap on the "plate.")*
This old man, he played nine,
*(Hold up nine fingers.)*
He played knick-knack on his spine.
*(Use index finger to point to spine.)*
This old man, he played ten,
*(Hold up ten fingers.)*
He played knick-knack now and then.
*(Using index finger, first point right, then point left.)*

# Bilateral Integration and Crossing the Midline *(cont.)*

Try each of the following activities that help develop bilateral integration and have students cross the midline. Introduce each activity by demonstrating it at a normal rate. Then, have the students follow along. Talk the students through each activity, slowing down the rate at which it is done. It is better to have students do a few repetitions well, rather than many repetitions quickly and sloppily. You may choose to have each student practice one side of the body before trying to alternate. As soon as the students have the idea of the activity repeat each motion in a sequence alternating from right to left. When the students are ready, have them do a sequence of five or ten. As students become skilled at performing each motion, increase the quantity.

- Hold a streamer in your right hand. Make large circles in front of the body. Then make circles while holding the streamer in your left hand.

- Lead with your right foot in a galloping motion. Then, lead with the left foot.

- Lift your right foot in front of the body so that you can touch it with the left hand. Put your foot back on the ground. Repeat with the left foot and the right hand.

- Reach your left hand behind the body to touch the right foot. Put your foot back on the ground. Repeat with the right hand and left foot.

- Stand up tall. Bend over and touch your right foot with your left hand. Repeat with the left foot and right hand.

- Toss a scarf or beanbag into the air with your right hand and catch it with the left hand.

- Touch your right knee with your left elbow. Put your foot back down on the ground. Repeat with the left knee and right elbow.

# Tactile Awareness

*Tactile awareness* refers to the student's sense of touch. Skin is the largest sensory area on our bodies. The palms of our hands and the bottoms of our feet are the most sensitive. We are constantly using our sense of touch for everything we do. Tactile receptors are located under the skin all over our bodies. Receptors in our hands help us to know whether an object is soft, hard, hot, cold, bumpy, smooth, etc. Tactile receptors also let us know when a breeze blows across our arms or legs. Tactile receptors in our mouths let us know if we have food in our mouths.

Students who are *tactile defensive*, or overly sensitive to touch, will be reluctant to touch many materials such as play dough, glue, finger paint, or other messy items. These students may also be very selective of what foods and textures they eat.

See page 12 for additional activities suitable for all children.

Below are some suggestions for helping students who are having difficulty with tactile awareness:

- Avoid approaching the student from the back; always let him or her see you approaching.

- Avoid unexpected touching of the student.

- Don't force, but encourage, participation in tactile activities.

- Encourage gradual exposure to messy experiences, even if only momentary.

- Encourage hand washing.

- Encourage student to pull and push heavy objects.

- Have the student go first or last in line so other students don't rub against him or her.

- Let him or her initiate touch.

- Let student have his or her own personal space when sitting on the floor, such as a carpet square.

- Let student rub various textures on his or her arms and legs.

- Offer a variety of manipulatives.

- Provide a variety of sensory experiences, such as a bean table, water table, or sand table.

- Provide an escape from too much sensation (i.e., a quiet corner).

- Use a firm touch on student's arms, legs, or back rather than a light touch.

# Tactile Awareness *(cont.)*

A good awareness of the sense of touch is an excellent place to begin when focusing on motor control activities. The activities on this page and the next develop children's kinesthetic awareness and refine their sense of touch.

## Texture Hunt

Review the various ways an object can feel (bumpy, smooth, rough, soft, or hard). Have students walk around the room touching a variety of objects. Challenge them to find one object that feels like each texture described.

Provide a variety of textures for students to touch. Be sure to include objects such as sandpaper, waxed paper, bubble wrap, a rock, pudding, oil, etc.

## Button Grab

Collect a variety of buttons and place them in a bag or box that students cannot see through. Have each student close his or her eyes and select two buttons out of the bag, placing one button in each hand. Have the child describe the shape of the button by using the sense of touch. Can the student tell which button is larger by touch alone?

## Banana Dig

Make a box of pudding according to the package directions. Put pudding in a small cup for each child. Slice the bananas and "hide" the slices in the pudding. Have students reach into the pudding in order to pull the bananas out and eat them. Begin by allowing students to have their eyes open. Then, have students close their eyes and find the bananas without looking.

**Teacher Note:** Handwashing prior to this activity and after is a must.

## Letter Writing

Pair students. Have each child write on the partner's back using his or her index finger. The student can draw shapes, or write letters, numbers, or words on his or her partner's back. Challenge the student whose back is being written on to figure out what has been written. Then, have the children switch places and do it again.

# Early Childhood Development

The accompanying developmental checklists suggest gross motor skills for children eighteen months through five years of age. The skills are arranged in groupings of several months at a time and are meant to be used as a guide rather than as a rigid timetable. This information will help you to anticipate stages of normal child development in the area of gross motor skills. Each child will acquire these skills at his or her own pace. Some children develop them more quickly in one area and more slowly in another. Consider creating a file folder for each child in which to keep the checklist, records, and anecdotal notes regarding the development noted in the student.

The toddler stage (eighteen months to three years old) is an exciting period of growth for children. They explore their environment using all five senses. They are the center of their universe, and the world revolves around them.

As children near the age of two, the experience does not have to become one of uncontrollable terror and mayhem. At this time, children are beginning to explore how much they can control their universe and what the limits are. The words "no" and "yes" become powerful ones, allowing them to take ownership of their own boundaries. With gentle guidance from parents and teachers, children can form limits of control that are compatible with the needs of others as well as their own.

Learning for a toddler often occurs when an activity can be repeated over and over. For example, a toddler loves to dump things out or over, put them back, and then do it again repeatedly. This simple activity is a challenge, and the child is striving to master it. There is delight in every accomplishment.

The preschooler (three-, four-, and five-year-olds) is becoming more autonomous. As he or she improves motor skills, the child is able to meet many needs with little help from an adult. Dressing, undressing, using the bathroom, and eating are some activities a preschooler can now do independently from an adult.

Preschoolers spend most of their time playing. Play is very important to their development. Play offers an excellent opportunity for language development. They enjoy playing in groups of peers, participating in dramatic play, and having a chance to stretch their imaginations.

A series of Gross Motor Skills Checklists can be found on pages 14–17. Of course, these are only guidelines. Every child has an individual pace and should not be compared to other children in general. Comparisons only become useful when a child's abilities are extremely disparate from others of his or her own age. Further investigation into the cause of such variances may be worthwhile. Be aware of differences, but do not jump to any conclusions. Most likely, any variance is within normal range.

# Gross Motor Skills Checklist

## Toddlers: 18 months to 24 months

**Child:** _____  **Date(s):** _____

Check all mastered gross motor skills.

❑ carries a large toy while walking

❑ runs stiffly

❑ sits in a small chair from a standing position by backing into it or sliding sideways

❑ walks backward

❑ walks upstairs with one hand held by an adult (both feet on step)

❑ stands on one foot momentarily with assistance

# Gross Motor Skills Checklist

**Child:** _____ **Date(s):** _____

Check all mastered gross motor skills.

- ❏ balances on a balance beam momentarily with both feet
- ❏ catches a large ball with arms and body
- ❏ climbs jungle gyms and ladders
- ❏ jumps backward
- ❏ jumps forward 6–18" (15–46 cm)
- ❏ jumps from bottom step to the floor
- ❏ jumps over a small object
- ❏ moves up and down a small slide independently
- ❏ pedals a tricycle 5–10' (1.5–3 m)
- ❏ runs a distance of 10' (3 m), avoiding obstacles
- ❏ stands on one foot for one to five seconds without assistance
- ❏ stands on one foot momentarily without assistance
- ❏ stands on tiptoes for several seconds
- ❏ throws a playground ball 5–7' (1.5–2.1 m)
- ❏ walks backward 10' (3 m)
- ❏ walks downstairs, alternating feet while holding the railing
- ❏ walks downstairs, holding railing with both feet on each step
- ❏ walks upstairs, alternating feet while holding the railing
- ❏ walks upstairs, holding railing with both feet on each step

# Gross Motor Skills Checklist

## Preschoolers: 36 months to 48 months

**Child:** _____  **Date(s):** _____

Check all mastered gross motor skills.

- ❑ avoids obstacles in path while running

- ❑ broad jumps over string or object 2" (5 cm) high

- ❑ gallops forward 10' (3 m)

- ❑ hops on one foot one time

- ❑ jumps forward a distance of 10" (25 cm)

- ❑ kicks a large ball that is rolling

- ❑ kicks a stationary ball

- ❑ pushes and pulls a wagon

- ❑ rides tricycle independently around corners

- ❑ runs on tiptoes

- ❑ throws a playground ball underhand to an adult

- ❑ walks on tiptoes 10' (3 m)

- ❑ walks upstairs, alternating feet without holding railing

# Gross Motor Skills Checklist

**Child:** _____ **Date(s):** _____

Check all mastered gross motor skills.

- ❏ attempts a somersault
- ❏ bounces ball two times and then catches it
- ❏ catches playground ball with both hands
- ❏ does forward somersaults independently
- ❏ hops on preferred foot for a distance of 2' (60 cm)
- ❏ jumps forward 10 times without falling
- ❏ jumps up 8–10" (20–25 cm)
- ❏ rides a "two-wheeler" with training wheels
- ❏ runs around objects/corners without falling
- ❏ skips five to ten seconds
- ❏ throws playground ball approximately 12' (3.6 m)
- ❏ throws small ball overhand 10–15' (3 m)
- ❏ walks down stairs, alternating feet without holding the railing
- ❏ walks heel-toe for 10' (3 m)
- ❏ walks on a low balance beam independently
- ❏ while swinging, pumps swing to sustain motion

# Helpful Hints
# for
# Gross Motor Skills
# Development

♦ Establish a signal which can be used to gain students' attention. This is especially useful when doing activities outdoors. The signal can be auditory, such as a whistle or horn, or it can be visual, such as two fingers held in the air or a red flash card.

♦ Determine the play space in which students will be working or playing. This is essential when conducting outdoor activities in order to gain the students' attention easily. Cones work well to mark the designated play area. If you do not have cones, make your own markers by spray-painting coffee cans and then filling them with sand.

♦ Demonstrate the action or activity as often as possible. Even if you are unable to demonstrate it, you can often find a student to use as an example as you guide him or her through the activity. Explain the rules of new outdoor games to the entire group in a confined area (the classroom is recommended) before going outside.

♦ When playing games, avoid situations where the children pick the teams. Arrange the teams so that they are equal in skill level.

♦ Choose activities that allow the children to be active most of the time. Set up multiple stations or have multiple activities from which students can choose if a particular activity lends itself to having only one child at a time participate.

♦ Have all of the equipment ready. If you do not have specific equipment for a game or activity, use the equipment on hand and improvise.

♦ Do not tolerate teasing or unsportsmanlike behavior. Set a high standard for student behavior when participating in activities. Be sure to establish and model what sportsmanlike behavior looks like. When students know what is expected, most students will emulate sportsmanlike behavior.

# Spatial and Body Awareness

*General space* is all the space within a room, or the boundary within which a student can move from an original starting point to another location. *Self space*, or *personal space*, is the immediate area surrounding a person. These concepts are important for children to learn since they teach the concept of personal boundaries. Once children understand the idea of personal and general space, they begin to comprehend the notions of boundaries and limits, and they can become proficient at the body control which is needed to succeed at a task within given limits.

*Body awareness* is the understanding of one's own potential for body movement and a sensitivity to one's physical being. For children, learning begins with the identification of body parts and the knowledge about the body's capacity for movement. As children develop motor skills and body awareness, they learn to use body parts effectively and competently in performing motor skills.

There are two ways that spatial and body awareness are addressed in this section: "Action Songs and Poems" and "Creative Movement." The "Action Songs and Poems" section contains the words and accompanying actions to original poems and traditional, well-loved, songs. The poems and songs were selected because students will use a variety of gross motor skills while performing the actions. The "Creative Movement" section provides activities that can be done with minimal or no materials. The activities were designed to get children moving in fun and creative ways.

## Hint

Be sure to define the space in which you will be conducting the activity. Students should know the boundaries in which they must move in order to participate in each activity. For students to understand the concept of personal space in the classroom, be very specific in your definition of what it is. For example, personal space may be a student's desk and chair, or perhaps just a chair. Each student should be cautioned not to invade another student's personal space during an activity which calls for using personal space.

# Action Songs and Poems

## Materials:

- kazoo (1 per child)
- hula hoop (1 per child)
- 3–4 beach towels
- fabric streamers (2 per child)

Teach the children the song, "The Wheels on the Bus." As students become familiar with the song and the actions, add props to make the song even more fun! Have children do the actions listed while singing the corresponding verse.

## The Wheels on the Bus

*(Lie down on one end of the road [beach towels laid lengthwise] and roll to the other end of the road. When you get to the other end of the road, pick up a hula hoop. As you sing, use the hoop as a steering wheel. Hold the hoop at 10 o'clock and 3 o'clock.)*

> The wheels on the bus go round and round,
> Round and round, round and round.
> The wheels on the bus go round and round,
> All through the town.

*(Place one streamer in each hand. Hold your arms in the air and wave both arms together back and forth like windshield wipers.)*

> The wipers on the bus go swish, swish, swish,
> Swish, swish, swish, swish, swish, swish.
> The wipers on the bus go swish, swish, swish,
> All through the town.

*(Sing and beep into the kazoo.)*

> The horn on the bus goes beep, beep, beep,
> Beep, beep, beep, beep, beep, beep.
> The horn on the bus goes beep, beep, beep,
> All through the town.

*(Hold your arms in front at shoulder level. Touch your thumb to the index and middle fingers and then open your hand back up to make a blinking motion.)*

> The lights on the bus go blink, blink, blink,
> Blink, blink, blink, blink, blink, blink.
> The lights on the bus go blink, blink, blink,
> All through the town.

*(Jump in place with your feet together.)*

> The children on the bus go bounce, bounce, bounce,
> Bounce, bounce, bounce, bounce, bounce, bounce.
> The children on the bus go bounce, bounce, bounce,
> All through the town.

---

**Directions for Making a Kazoo:** Use a paper hole punch to make one hole 1" (2.54 cm) down from the end of a toilet-paper tube. Place a piece of waxed paper on the same end and secure it with a rubber band about ³/₄" (2 cm) from the end.

---

# Action Songs and Poems (cont.)

## Materials:

- none

Teach students the poems below and then show them actions to go with each animal. Once the poem is over, have each student choose his or her favorite animal and do actions that correspond to that animal. Extend this poem by helping students change the verses. Substitute another animal in each appropriate line.

## Animal Show

It's time for the animal, animal show.

Leap like a frog and go, go, go.

Buzz like a bumblebee, little owls hoot.

Run like a baby fox, cute, cute, cute.

It's time for the animal, animal show.

Crawl like a turtle and go, go, go.

Spin like a spider and sing like a bird.

Prettiest song you've ever heard.

It's time for the animal, animal show.

Choose your favorite animal and go, go, go!

## Looby Lou

Here we go looby lou,
*(Children hold hands and sway them gently.)*

Here we go looby lie,

Here we go looby lou,

All on a Saturday night.

You put your right hand in,
*(Put right hand in the circle.)*

You put your right hand out,

*(Put right hand outside the circle.)*

You give your right hand a shake, shake, shake,
*(Shake your hand.)*

And turn yourself about.
*(Turn around in a circle.)*

*(Repeat substituting the following body parts for "right hand:" left hand, right leg, left leg, head, whole self.)*

# Action Songs and Poems *(cont.)*

**Materials:**

- paintbrush or paint roller (1 per child)

While singing the song below, have each child touch body parts as he or she sings or says the words.

## Head, Shoulders, Knees, and Toes

Head, shoulders, knees, and toes,

Knees and toes.

Head, shoulders, knees, and toes,

Knees and toes.

Eyes and ears,

And mouth and nose.

Head, shoulders, knees, and toes,

Knees and toes.

### Variation

When the child is comfortable with the song, give him or her a paintbrush or paint roller. Sing the song again, this time slower. As you sing about each body part, the child "paints" with the paint roller or paintbrush on the appropriate spot. Begin by practicing on the leg before starting the song.

# Action Songs and Poems *(cont.)*

## Materials:

- beanbag or hula hoop (1 per child)

Have children form a circle before beginning the song. Start by teaching children the words and the actions that go with the song. Once students have become familiar with the song, give them something to balance on their bodies during each verse. For example, give each student a beanbag. The student can hold the beanbag in his or her hands, or balance the bean bag on his or her shoes or head.

## Hokey Pokey

You put your right hand in,

*(Put right hand in the circle.)*

You put your right hand out,

*(Move right hand out of the circle.)*

You put your right hand in,

*(Put right hand in the circle.)*

And you shake it all about.

*(Shake your hand.)*

You do the Hokey Pokey and you turn yourself around,

*(Hold your palms out in front and wave, then turn around.)*

That's what it's all about.

*(Clap two times.)*

You do the Hokey Pokey,
You do the Hokey Pokey,
You do the Hokey Pokey.
That's what it's all about!

*(Repeat for each verse, substituting with a different body part.)*

You put your left hand in, etc.
You put your right foot in, etc.
You put your left foot in, etc.
You put your head in, etc.
Your put your whole self in, etc.

# Action Songs and Poems *(cont.)*

**Materials:**

- none

Have children form a large circle. Number the children to 10 (as many times as needed) so that everyone has a number. Have the children sing the song below. As each child's number is sung, he or she takes five steps toward the middle of the circle and turns to face the outside of the circle. When the child's number is sung during the second verse, he or she walks back to his or her original place in the circle. **Note:** If appropriate, hand out number cards for each of the 10 children.

The word *apples* can be replaced with a word for the theme you are currently studying. For example, you could sing about "Ten Little Squirrels" or "Ten Little Penguins."

### Ten Little Apples

One little, two little, three little apples,

Four little, five little, six little apples,

Seven little, eight little, nine little apples,

Ten little apples on the tree.

Ten little, nine little, eight little apples,

Seven little, six little, five little apples,

Four little, three little, two little apples,

One little apple on the ground.

# Action Songs and Poems (cont.)

**Materials:**

- none

Teach the students the following poems.  Then, as you chant the words together, have them act out the words.  Once students are familiar with these poems, create poem innovations together.  Try writing, "Run, Little Cheetah" or "A Day at the Beach" together.  Ask the students to demonstrate how their motions for these new poems will differ.

## Swim, Little Fishies

Little fishies swim and

Little fishies glide.

Little fishies jump and

Little fishies dive.

Swim, little fishies,

One, two, three, four.

Turn yourselves around and

Swim some more.

## A Day in the Snow

Let's get ready for a day in the snow.

One, two, three, it's time to go.

Put on your coat and put on your hat.

Put on your gloves as easy as that.

Slide through the snow.

Throw snow in the air.

Let those snowflakes fall in your hair.

Burr!  I'm cold.  It's time to go.

What a great day we had playing in the snow!

# Action Songs and Poems *(cont.)*

**Materials:**

- small stickers (about 10 per child)

Begin by teaching children the words and the actions that accompany the poems/songs. Once students become familiar with the songs, provide small stickers that they can use to place on the body parts mentioned in each poem. Give students directions where to place each sticker. (For example, "Put one sticker on your left shoulder.") Have each student place a sticker on the body parts mentioned in the poem. When the student recites the poem, have him or her use the index finger to touch the stickers.

**Teacher Note:** Have students place stickers under their eyes and mouths instead of directly on them.

## On My Head

On my head, my hands I place.

On my shoulders, my hands I place.

On my face, my hands I place.

On my hips, my hands I place.

And at my side, my hands I place.

Then behind me they will hide.

I will hold them up so high.

Quickly make my fingers fly.

Hold them out in front of me.

Swiftly clap—one, two, three.

## Hands on Shoulders

Hands on shoulders, hands on knees,

Hands behind you if you please.

Touch your shoulders, now your nose,

Now your chin and now your toes.

Hands up high as can be,

Down at your side and touch your knee.

Hands up high as before,

Now clap your hands—one, two, three, four.

# Action Songs and Poems *(cont.)*

**Materials:**

- small stickers (about 10 per child)

Have each student place a sticker on the body parts mentioned in the poem. When the student recites the poem, have him or her use the index finger to touch the stickers.

**Teacher Note:** Have students place stickers under their eyes and mouths instead of directly on them.

## I Have a Nose

On my face I have a nose.
*(Touch nose with one finger.)*

And way down here I have ten toes.
*(Bend over and touch toes with both hands.)*

I have two eyes that I can blink.
*(Point to both eyes with both fingers.)*

I have a head to help me think.
*(Touch head with one finger.)*

I have a chin and very near,
*(Touch chin with one finger.)*

I have two ears to help me hear.
*(Touch both ears with both fingers.)*

I have a mouth with which to speak.
*(Point to mouth with one finger.)*

And when I run I use my feet.
*(Tap feet.)*

Here are arms to hold up high.
*(Hold up both arms.)*

And here's a hand to wave good-bye.
*(Wave with one hand.)*

# Action Songs and Poems *(cont.)*

**Materials:**

- colored electrical or masking tape (or 1 carpet square per child)

Mark off squares (12" or 30 cm on each side) on the carpet with colored electrical or masking tape. Have each child stand in a square. Teach the action poems, "Good Night" and "I Can Jump." Encourage the child to stay in his or her square while performing the actions to these songs. This action will require a lot of balance and body control.

## Good Night

Two little hands go clap, clap, clap.
*(Clap hands.)*

Two little arms lie in my lap.
*(Lay arms in lap.)*

Two little feet go bump, bump, bump.
*(Bump feet.)*

Two little legs give one big jump.
*(Jump one time.)*

Two little eyes are shut up tight.
*(Shut eyes.)*

One little voice whispers a soft,
"Good night."
*(Whisper, "Good night.")*

## I Can Jump

I can jump, jump, jump.

I can hop, hop, hop.

I can clap, clap, clap.

I can stop, stop, stop.

I can nod my head for "yes."

I can shake my head for "no."

I can bend my knees a little bit.

And sit—down—slow!

# Action Songs and Poems *(cont.)*

**Materials:**

• beanbag (1 per child)

After students become familiar with the words to both versions of the "Teddy Bear Song," challenge each student to perform the actions in the songs while balancing a bean bag on his or her head. Another animal or person may be substituted for the word teddy bear. Consider any themes you are teaching and upcoming holidays. For example, the song could be about a scarecrow during the fall.

## Teddy Bear Song

Teddy bear, teddy bear, turn around.

Teddy bear, teddy bear, touch the ground.

Teddy bear, teddy bear, reach up high.

Teddy bear, teddy bear, touch the sky.

Teddy bear, teddy bear, bend down low.

Teddy bear, teddy bear, touch your toe.

## Teddy Bear Song
(Alternate Version)

Teddy bear, teddy bear, turn around.

Teddy bear, teddy bear, touch the ground.

Teddy bear, teddy bear, go upstairs.

Teddy bear, teddy bear, brush your hair.

Teddy bear, teddy bear, turn out the light.

Teddy bear, teddy bear, say good night.

# Action Songs and Poems *(cont.)*

## Materials:

- none

These are two well-loved, traditional rhymes students should learn. Teach students the movements to these songs and allow them to practice. Then, once students are familiar with the songs, have them sing the songs using different voices. For example, a student can sing, "I'm a Little Tea Pot," using a silly voice or a fast-singing voice. Have students sing the rhymes using some of the following "voices."

- Silly Voice
- Super Slow Voice
- Fast Voice
- Sweet Voice
- Slow Voice
- Baby Voice
- Angry Voice

## London Bridge

London Bridge is falling down,
falling down, falling down.

London Bridge is falling down, my fair lady.

Take the keys and lock her up,
lock her up, lock her up.

Take the keys and lock her up, my fair lady.

*(Two students face each other. Students place their palms against each other and raise their arms over their heads as if making a bridge. Another set of students makes a line and walks under the bridge. The students making the bridge lower their arms to capture a student between them during the line, "Take the keys and lock her up. . ." Gently sway the captured student back and forth until the poem is complete. Repeat.)*

## I'm a Little Teapot

I'm a little teapot short and stout.
*(Bend your knees slightly and hold your hands out to the side.)*

Here is my handle,
*(Left hand holds hip.)*

Here is my spout.
*(Point your fingers on right hand down and hold arm out to make a spout.)*

When I get all steamed up hear me shout,

Just tip me over and pour me out.
*(Lean over slightly to the right.)*

# Action Songs and Poems *(cont.)*

**Materials:**

- none

### If You're Happy and You Know It

If you're happy and you know it, clap your hands.
*(Clap, clap.)*

If you're happy and you know it, clap your hands.
*(Clap, clap.)*

If you're happy and you know it, then your face will surely show it.
If you're happy and you know it, clap your hands.
*(Clap, clap.)*

*(Continue in the same manner substituting the following for "clap your hands": "stomp your feet," "shout hurrah," and "do all three.")*

Once children know and are familiar with the words to "If You're Happy and You Know It," create some additional verses to go with the song. For example:

- If you're silly and you know it, make a face.

- If you're grumpy and you know it, cross your arms.

- If you're angry and you know it, stomp your feet.

- If you're confused and you know it, scratch your head.

- If you're frustrated and you know it, kick the dirt.

### Who Feels Happy?

Who feels happy? Who feels glad today?

All who do clap their hands this way.

Who feels happy? Who feels glad today?

All who do nod their heads this way.

*(After students are able to easily do the nodding action in "Who Feels Happy," continue adding body parts such as "stomp their feet this way" or "with your mouth, shout hurray!")*

# Action Songs and Poems *(cont.)*

## Materials:

- none

Take students outside on a nice sunny day. Guide them to notice their shadows. Be sure to give plenty of time for students to play with their shadows. Gather students together and recite the poem for them while they listen. Then, recite the poem again as the children and their shadows follow along. Students love this poem and you will probably have to recite it several times.

### What Is a Shadow?

If I walk, my shadow walks.

If I run, my shadow runs.

And when I stand still, as you can see,

My shadow stands beside me.

When I hop, my shadow hops.

When I jump, my shadow jumps.

And when I stand still, as you can see,

My shadow sits beside me.

### Clap Your Hands and Wiggle Your Toes

*(To the Tune of: "Twinkle, Twinkle, Little Star")*

Clap your hands and wiggle your toes,

That's the way this silly song goes.

Wink one eye, lift hands high.

Now it's time to say, "Good-bye."

Clap your hands and wiggle your toes,

That's the way this silly song goes.

32 ©Teacher Created Materials, Inc.

# Action Songs and Poems *(cont.)*

## Materials:

- binoculars (1 pair per child)

Teach the children the poem, "Bear Hunt." Allow each child to make a pair of binoculars to take with him or her on the bear hunt. Stop between verses and have the student raise the binoculars to the eyes to look for bears. Maybe the binoculars will help the student spot the bear sooner!

## Bear Hunt

I'm going on a bear hunt.

*(Slap thighs.)*

I see a swamp.

*(Hold hands as if looking.)*

Can't go under it,

*(Swoop hands down low.)*

Can't go over it,

*(Hold hands high.)*

Have to go through it.

Slush, slush, slush, slush, slush.

*(Rub hands together.)*

I'm going on a bear hunt.

I see a bridge.

Can't go under it,

Can't go through it,

Have to go over it.

Thump, thump, thump, thump, thump.

*(Pound chest.)*

I'm going on a bear hunt.

I see a stream.

Can't go under it,

Can't go over it,

Have to go through it.

Splash, splash, splash, splash, splash.

*(Swimming strokes.)*

I'm going on a bear hunt.

I see a tree.

Can't go under it,

Can't go through it,

Have to go up it.

Up, up, up, up, up.

*(Fingers climb up.)*

Down, down, down, down, down.

*(Fingers climb down.)*

I'm going on a bear hunt.

I see a cave.

Can't go over it,

Can't go under it,

Have to go through it.

I feel something.

*(Feel with hands.)*

I feel something furry.

It feels like a bear.

It looks like a bear.

It is a bear!

Run!

Up the tree.

Down the tree.

Splash, splash, splash.

Thump, thump, thump.

Slush, slush, slush.

WOO!

## Directions for Making Binoculars

Glue two toilet-paper tubes together and allow them to dry. Punch a hole on each side of the toilet-paper tubes that are not glued together. Tie the end of a piece of yarn to each of the holes forming a necklace. Allow each student to decorate his or her binoculars.

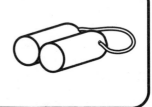

# Action Songs and Poems *(cont.)*

## Materials:

- a small ball (1 per child)

You may want to teach students the song, "Have You Ever Seen a Lassie?" before teaching them, "Have You Ever Seen a Penguin?" Once students are familiar with the song, teach them the actions that go with it. Provide each student with a small ball. The student places the ball between his or her knees and holds it there while doing the actions to this song. (It will really make them look like they are waddling!)

The word *penguin* and the actions that go with a penguin can be replaced with any theme or animal you are currently studying in the classroom.

## Have You Ever Seen a Penguin?

*(To the Tune of: "Have You Ever Seen a Lassie?")*

Have you ever seen a penguin,

a penguin, a penguin?

Have you ever seen a penguin swim this way and that?

Swim this way and that way

and this way and that way?
*(Make swimming motions with your arms.)*

Have you ever seen a penguin swim this way and that?

Repeat, substituting these words for "swim":

- slide

  *(Make sliding motions with hands and feet.)*

- waddle

  *(Take tiny little steps, swinging your body right and left.)*

- dress

  *(Boys bow and girls curtsy.)*

# Action Songs and Poems *(cont.)*

## Materials:

- none

The simple, repetitive words to this song make it easy for children to learn. Begin by having children sit on the floor, with their backs straight, knees bent, feet on the floor, and fists resting on their sides. Teach students the actions to the songs as you demonstrate. Challenge each student to think of how he or she could extend the song by having Jenny work with six or seven hammers. Encourage them to think of other parts of their bodies that they could use, and help them to create additional verses.

## The Hammer

Jenny works with one hammer, one hammer, one hammer.

*(Bring one fist up and down beside you, bending at the elbow.)*

Jenny works with one hammer.

Then she works with two.

Jenny works with two hammers, two hammers, two hammers.

*(Bring both fists up and down, on either side of you.)*

Jenny works with two hammers.

Then she works with three.

Jenny works with three hammers, three hammers, three hammers.

*(Bring both fists up on either side of you and bring one foot up and down in front of you.)*

Jenny works with three hammers.

Then she works with four.

Jenny works with four hammers, four hammers, four hammers.

*(Bring both fists and both feet up and down.)*

Jenny works with four hammers.

Then she works with five.

Jenny works with five hammers, five hammers, five hammers.

*(Bring both fists and feet up and down and nod your head up and down.*

Jenny works with five hammers. Then she goes to sleep!

*(Roll over on your side and pretend to sleep.)*

# Action Songs and Poems *(cont.)*

**Materials:**

- none

Arrange students in a large circle. Number the children to 10 (as many times as needed so that each child has a number). Have the children sing the song, "The Ants Go Marching." As a child's number is sung, he or she marches into the middle of the circle. As the verse is coming to a close, the child marches back to his or her place in the circle. The rest of the students can march in place in the circle while they are waiting for their turns.

## The Ants Go Marching

*(To the Tune of: "When Johnny Comes Marching Home")*

The ants go marching *one by one*,

Hurrah, hurrah!

The ants go marching *one by one*,

Hurrah, hurrah!

The ants go marching *one by one*,

The little one stops to *suck his thumb*,

And they all go marching down

in the ground to get out of the rain,

Boom! Boom! Boom!

*(Use the following phrases for subsequent verses, replacing the italicized text above.)*

- *Two by two, tie his shoe.*
- *Three by three, climb a tree.*
- *Four by four, shut the door.*
- *Five by five, take a dive.*
- *Six by six, pick up sticks.*
- *Seven by seven, wave to heaven.*
- *Eight by eight, shut the gate.*
- *Nine by nine, check the time.*
- *Ten by ten, say, "The end."*

# Action Songs and Poems *(cont.)*

**Materials:**

- a stuffed animal (1 per student)

Provide a stuffed animal for each student or have the student bring in his or her favorite stuffed animal from home. After students are able to perform the songs/poems with the actions, have each student use his or her stuffed animal to perform the actions. The student moves the stuffed animal's arms and legs in order to complete the songs and poem.

## Gathering Song

*(To the Tune of: "Skip to My Lou")*

Come, come, sit on the floor.
*(Pat the floor next to you.)*
Come, come, sit on the floor.
Come, come, sit on the floor.
Sit on the floor and sing.

Clap, clap, clap your hands.
*(Clap your hands.)*
Clap, clap, clap your hands.
Clap, clap, clap your hands.
Clap your hands and sing.

Touch, touch, touch your nose.
*(Touch your nose.)*
Touch, touch, touch your nose.
Touch, touch, touch your nose.
Touch your nose with me.

## Hands Up

Reach for the ceiling, touch the floor.
Stand up again, let's do more.
Touch your head,
'Then your knees.
Go to your shoulder like this. See?
Reach for the ceiling,
Touch the floor.
That's all now. There isn't any more.

# Action Songs and Poems *(cont.)*

**Materials:**

- 3' (91 cm) dowel  (1 per fishing pole)
- string
- construction paper
- paperclips
- doughnut magnet

Have students go fishing while reciting the poem below.  (See page 205 for directions.)

## I Caught a Fish Alive

One, two, three, four, five,

*(Hold up each of five fingers, one at a time.)*

I caught a fish alive.

*(Pretend to hold a fish.)*

Six, seven, eight, nine, ten,

*(Raise up fingers of other hand, one at a time.)*

I let it go again.

*(Pretend to throw the fish back.)*

Why did I let it go?

*(Hold up your hands, looking puzzled.)*

Because it bit my finger so!

*(Shake right hand.)*

Which finger did it bite?

*(Hold up right hand.)*

The little one on the right.

*(Point to your pinkie.)*

# Action Songs and Poems *(cont.)*

**Materials:**

- pillows, mats, or foam pads

Arrange students in groups of five. Have each group stand in a circle holding hands. Students can act out, "Five Little Monkeys." Add to the fun by providing students with pillows, mats, or foam pads that the students can jump on while acting out the story. As each monkey falls, one student in the group sits down.

## Five Little Monkeys

Five little monkeys jumping on the bed,

One fell off and broke his head.

Mama called the doctor, and the doctor said,

"No more monkeys jumping on the bed."

Four little monkeys jumping on the bed,

One fell off and broke his head.

Mama called the doctor, and the doctor said,

"No more monkeys jumping on the bed."

Three little monkeys jumping on the bed,

One fell off and broke his head.

Mama called the doctor and the doctor said,

"No more monkeys jumping on the bed."

Two little monkeys jumping on the bed,

One fell off and broke his head.

Mama called the doctor and the doctor said,

"No more monkeys jumping on the bed."

One little monkey jumping on the bed,

One fell off and broke his head.

Mama called the doctor and the doctor said,

"No more monkeys jumping on the bed."

# Creative Movement

## Materials:

- large area where children can lie down

## Shapes

Explain to students that this is a game in which they will demonstrate geometric shapes: circle, square, rectangle, and triangle. When they hear the name of a shape, students will get into a group and form the correct figure. To form a triangle, they will get into groups of three; a square, groups of four; a rectangle, groups of six; and a circle, any number of students. At a signal, the teacher will name one of these geometric shapes. Students will get into appropriately-sized groups to form the shape given. Any students left without a partner will make the shape by himself or herself.

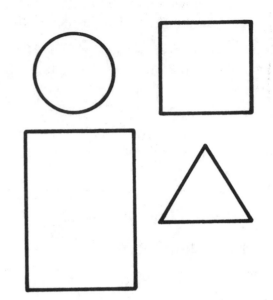

## Body Letters

Encourage students to create the letters of the alphabet with their bodies. (See this page and pages 41–44.) Some letters can be made by an individual student, while other letters will require students to work together. Call out a letter of the alphabet. Have each student determine if the letter can be made alone or if they will need the help of a friend. Students place their bodies in a position so that the letter of the alphabet is shown.

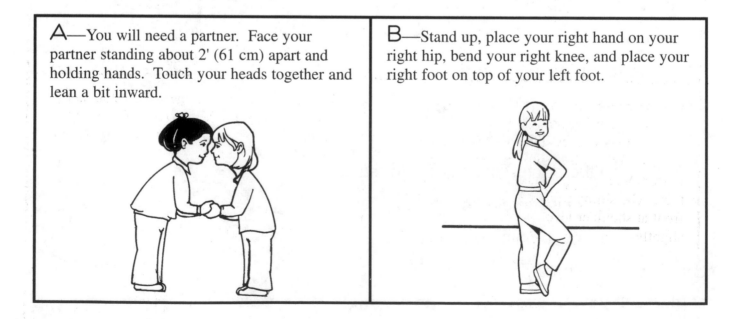

A—You will need a partner. Face your partner standing about 2' (61 cm) apart and holding hands. Touch your heads together and lean a bit inward.

B—Stand up, place your right hand on your right hip, bend your right knee, and place your right foot on top of your left foot.

# Creative Movement *(cont.)*

C—Sit down on the floor and with your arms over your head, bend your body slightly over your legs.

D—You will need a partner. One student stands up straight. The other student faces the first, putting his or her hands on the first student's shoulders. The second student places his or her toes against the straight-standing student's toes and bends slightly at the waist and leans back keeping his or her head between the arms.

E—Sit on the floor with your legs straight out in front of you. Hold your left arm straight out in front of you at shoulder level. Bend your right arm. Hold your elbow into your body with your fingers extended out in front.

F—Stand up, hold your left arm straight out in front of you at shoulder level. Bend your right arm at the elbow, and place your elbow on your waist with your fingers pointed straight out in front of you.

G—You will need a partner. One student stands up, putting both arms over his or her head and leans over slightly. The second student sits on the floor with legs straight out in front and feet touching the first student's toes. The sitting person then puts arms out in front at shoulder level and leans forward slightly.

H—You will need a partner. Two students stand next to each other about 2' (61 cm) apart. Join inside hands, keeping your elbows next to your sides.

# Creative Movement *(cont.)*

I—Stand up tall with your feet together and your toes pointed outward to the side. Put hands on your chin, bring your elbows up to shoulder level and out to the side.

J—You will need a partner. One partner stands up straight. The second partner sits to the side of the first partner. The second partner's feet touch the side of the first partner's right foot.

K—Stand up straight. Lift your right leg up and don't bend your knee. Put your elbow on your waist and hold your hand in front of you pointing up.

L—Kneel on the floor and keep your upper body straight and tall.

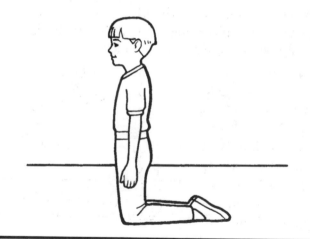

M—You will need a partner. Stand next to each other about 2' (61 cm) apart and hold hands.

N—You will need a partner. One partner stands on one foot and bends the other leg at the knee so the foot is up in the air pointing to the other partner. The second partner holds the first partner's raised foot with his or her hand.

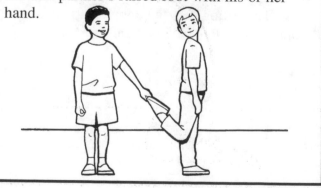

42          ©Teacher Created Materials, Inc.

# Creative Movement *(cont.)*

O—You will need a partner. One partner sits on the floor with his or her legs straight out in front. The second partner stands in front of the first partner and places his or her hands on the first partner's head. The second partner's feet go next to the first partner's feet.

P—Stand up tall. Take your right hand and touch your forehead.

Q—You will need a partner. One partner sits on the floor with his or her legs straight out in front of his or her body, leans back slightly with arms straightened out behind his or her back. The second partner stands in front of the first partner, touching the first partner's feet with his or her feet, and places his or her hands on the first partner's head.

R—Stand up tall. Bend your right elbow and touch your head. Keeping your knee stiff, raise your right leg.

S—Kneel down. Bring both arms over your head and lean forward slightly.

T—Stand up tall. Hold both arms straight out to the side at shoulder level.

# Creative Movement *(cont.)*

U—You will need a partner. Both partners kneel on the floor so their toes are touching and their bodies are upright.

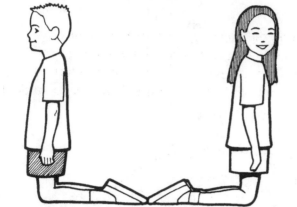

V—Sit down on the floor. Bring both legs up together, keeping knees straight. Balance by placing your hands at your sides.

W—You will need three students. The first student stands and then bends at the waist and touches the floor with his or her hands. One student kneels by the first student's feet. The third student kneels by the first student's hands.

X—You will need a partner. Stand back-to-back. Both partners should move their feet slightly forward and both should lean slightly forward.

Y—Stand up tall. Hold both your arms out and above your head.

Z—Kneel on the floor. Put both arms out in front of you at shoulder level and lean back slightly.

44    ©Teacher Created Materials, Inc.

# Creative Movement *(cont.)*

## Materials:

- none

## Imagine That!

Get students' imaginations going by having them pantomime the creative movement activities listed below. You can have the whole class participate at the same time or turn the activity into a game by having one child pantomime each activity while the other students guess. If you choose to turn the activity into a game, write each movement on an index card for students to choose from. For a student who cannot read yet, you may whisper the movement into his or her ear.

- build a building with blocks
- climb a ladder
- climb a tree
- climb up and down a ladder
- dance slowly, then quickly
- deal cards
- deliver the mail
- dig a hole with a shovel
- erase the chalkboard
- hammer nails
- hang up laundry on a clothesline
- ice skate
- juggle
- march like you are a soldier
- paddle downstream
- play hopscotch
- play the guitar
- pop like popcorn
- put a key in a treasure chest and open it
- put on a coat
- put on an apron
- put on gloves
- scoop ice cream
- shoot an arrow
- sizzle like bacon
- swing an ax
- wrap a gift

# Creative Movement *(cont.)*

## Materials:

- none

## Move Like This

Encourage a variety of movement activities by giving commands for students to follow. Begin with simple commands. As students become skilled at performing the simple commands, begin making the commands more complex. Incorporate a variety of movements in your complex commands including: clapping, tapping feet, jumping, hopping, marching, moving forward and backward, spinning around, and lifting hands, arms, knees, legs, and feet. Use the following and make up some of your own:

- bounce up and down, quickly then slowly

- clap your hands over your head one time

- clap your hands quickly, then slowly

- do five jumping jacks

- drag your feet around the room

- hop forward, backward, and sideways

- jump high

- jump nine times

- lean left, right, forward, and backward

- lift your left arm, left leg, and left hand at the same time

- move your right and left elbows up and down and then in forward and backward circles

- move your right and left shoulders up and down slowly, then quickly

- pat your head and stomach

- quickly jump on your right foot, on your left foot, on both feet, then stop

- step, walk, hop, and jump backward

- tap your feet softly, loudly, slowly, then quickly

- touch your toes

- walk backward

- whirl around

# Creative Movement *(cont.)*

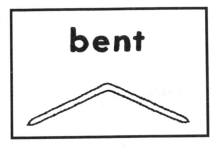

## Materials:

- pipe-cleaner figure (See page 48 for directions.)
- Sight Word Movement Cards
  (See pages 49–50 for directions.)

## Pipe Cleaner Body Movement

Before introducing the pipe-cleaner figures, have students demonstrate some of the following movements using their bodies. For example, "Our bodies can make interesting shapes. Our bodies can be straight. Can you show your body making a straight shape? What part of your body is making a straight shape? Can you find a different way to make a straight shape? Show me. Our bodies can make curved shapes. Please show me a way that your body can make a curved shape. What part of your body is making the curved shape?"

Introduce the three Sight Word Movement Cards *(straight, bent, curved)*. Hold up one card at a time and discuss the meaning of the word. Have students move their bodies to demonstrate each word. Repeat until students have found several body positions for each type of movement.

Provide each child with a pipe-cleaner figure. Hold up each Movement Card again, one at a time. Have the student first demonstrate the movement with his or her body, then manipulate the pipe-cleaner figure to demonstrate the word. Repeat until the student has found several ways to demonstrate each movement.

Reverse the process by having each student manipulate his or her pipe-cleaner figure to demonstrate a word, then try to see if he or she can copy the pipe-cleaner figure with his or her own body. The student will discover that sometimes he or she can not make the same figure. (Our bodies are not quite as flexible as a pipe-cleaner figure!) Place two of the Movement Cards in plain view. State the two words. Ask students, "Can you make a shape with your body that uses both a straight and a curved shape? What part of your body is making the curved shape and the straight shape?"

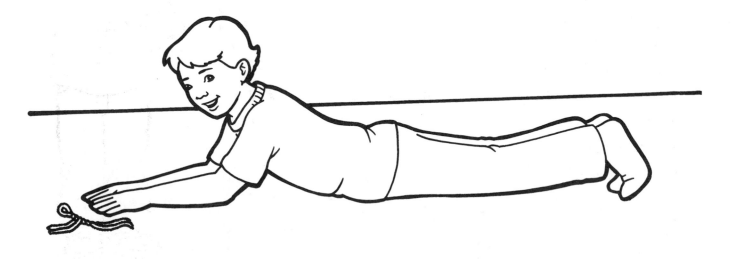

# Creative Movement *(cont.)*

## Materials:

- one 12" (30 cm) red pipe cleaner
- one 12" (30 cm) white pipe cleaner
- one 4½" (11.5 cm) white pipe cleaner

## Pipe-Cleaner Figure

1. Hold the 12" (30 cm) red and white pipe cleaners side by side. From the bottom, measure up 5" (13 cm). At this point, twist the pipe cleaners together above the 5" for the next 3½" (9 cm) for a candy cane look.

2. Form legs by separating the bottom 5" (13 cm) lengths into an upside-down "v" and bending the ends of the pipe cleaners to form feet.

3. With the remaining 3½" (9 cm) above the twisted area, bend the red pipe cleaner outward so the red "arm" is parallel with the red "leg." Repeat with the white pipe cleaner to form the other arm. Bend the ends of the arms to form hands.

4. Using the 4½" (11.5 cm) pipe cleaner, twist the ends to form an oval head and attach it to the pipe-cleaner body at the point where the arms extend from the body.

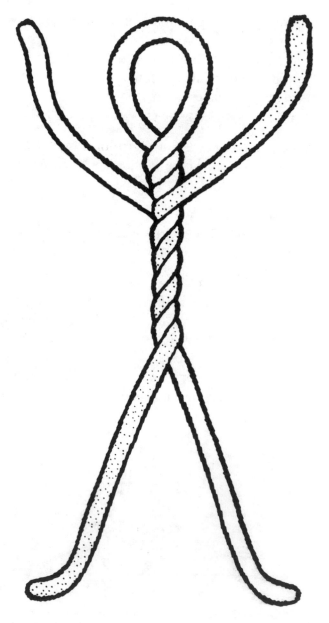

# Creative Movement *(cont.)*

## Materials:

- Sight Word Movement Cards (this page and the next page)
- three 12" (30 cm) red pipe cleaners
- one black permanent marker
- glue

## Sight Word Movement Cards

1. Copy the Movement Cards onto cardstock.

2. Bend the pipe cleaners, one per word, to match the drawings and visually represent the three shapes.

3. Glue each of the pipe cleaners on top of the drawing on the respective card; allow to dry. An alternative is to simply color the drawing of the pipe cleaner rather than gluing a pipe cleaner to the card.

bent

# Creative Movement (cont.)

## Sight Word Movement Cards (cont.)

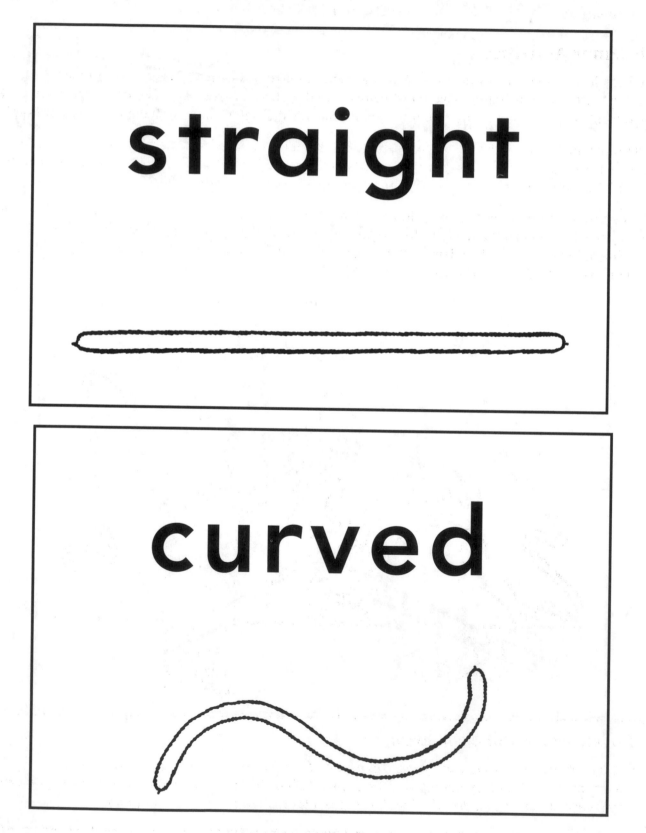

# Creative Movement *(cont.)*

## Materials:

- streamers
- dowel (optional)
- stapler

## Streamer Activities

Students love to play with streamers.  Making them available is one of the fastest ways to get them moving.  After demonstrating what the streamers are designed for, you can make the streamers available for students to play with during free time, guide students through some movement activities, or both!

Determine the length of the streamers based on the height of the students and how much experience they have with using streamers.  Shorter streamers (approximately 2' or 61 cm ) are easier to control; longer streamers (longer than 3' or 91 cm) require more control.

The first time you introduce students to using streamers, you will want to allow them time to free play.  Don't expect students to be ready to follow verbal cues unless they have had sufficient time to experiment.  Once you feel students will be focused enough to follow some verbal directions, try some of the movement activities provided on pages 52–55.

### Directions for Making a Streamer

Cut lengths of paper streamers (these can usually be purchased at party supply stores).  Or, streamers can be made by cutting lengths of fabric about 3" (8 cm) in width.  If you wish, you can staple each streamer to a dowel.  The dowel provides a place for the student to hold.

# Creative Movement (cont.)

## Materials:

- streamers (2 per child)

## Basic Streamer Movements

Listed below are some basic movements that can be done with streamers. Before you try giving the students verbal directions, you will want to provide them with a few minutes of free time to experiment with the streamers. Allow the students to get the "wiggles" out first. Begin with each student holding only one streamer. Then, as the student is able to control the streamer better, provide another streamer for him or her to try the same activities using both hands.

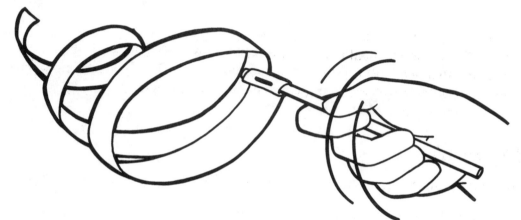

## Suggested Progression for Movements

- Using either hand, make small circles on the side of your body, clockwise, then counterclockwise.

- Using only your left hand, make small circles on the side of your body. First move in a clockwise direction, then counterclockwise.

- Using only your right hand, make small circles on the side of your body. First move in a clockwise direction, then counterclockwise.

- Using both hands, make small circles on the sides of your body. First move in a clockwise direction, then counterclockwise.

- Repeat the activities above, altering the following:

- Make large circles on the sides of the body.

- Make small circles in front of the body.

- Make large circles in front of the body.

- Make large circles in front of the body, touching the tummy with the hand each time you pass it.

- Make small circles in front of the body, touching the tummy with the hand each time you pass it.

- Reach to the floor and then up high to the ceiling.

- Reach to the floor and then up high to the ceiling while making circles with your hands.

# Creative Movement *(cont.)*

## Materials:

- streamers (2 per child)
- music

## Streamer Pantomime

Provide each student with two streamers, one for each hand. After allowing some time for free play and experimentation, try some of the following movement activities with your children.

## Music

Play a variety of music. Ask the students to adjust their movements to go along with the beat of the music. Experiment by playing classical music, rock and roll, jazz, blues, hard rock, etc. After participating in moving to at least three different types of music, ask students to describe how their movements changed as the music changed. How did they know how quickly or slowly to move? Which kind of music did they like most?

## Suggested Movements

Ask students to use their imaginations to demonstrate some of the movements listed below:

- Be a snowflake fluttering slowly down, twirling around.

- Be a butterfly flying through the air.

- Be a fish swimming in the sea.

- Be a bolt of lightning shooting down.

- Be a bird flying to his nest.

- Be the wind blowing all about.

- Be a wave crashing on the shore.

# Creative Movement *(cont.)*

## Materials:

- streamers (2 per child)

## Streamer Stories

Provide each child with two streamers, one for each hand. Tell a story by reading the suggestions below, or creating your own by elaborating on some of the movements listed below and on the following page. As you tell them a story, direct the students to move accordingly. Be sure to ask students to use their imaginations.

### ✱ Sprouting

Pretend you are a seed. Curl your body up tightly so that you can be planted in the ground. Water is being sprinkled on you and you begin to grow, slowly at first, then faster. Suddenly, you pop up out of the ground and are a sprout. Leaves begin to grow as your stem gets taller. Finally, a flower blooms at the top of the plant.

### ✱ A Storm

Pretend you are a tree. Your body is the trunk and your arms and hands are the branches. It is a nice, sunny day with a gentle breeze. Suddenly, a storm approaches. The wind begins to blow a little harder, a little harder, a little harder. You realize that you are in a hurricane. The wind blows wildly around you and then begins to slowly die down. As the wind stops blowing, the sun comes out. Birds begin to build a nest in the branches of the tree.

### ✱ Growing

Pretend you are a caterpillar. You are very hungry. You search all over for food to eat. When you become full, you find a safe branch on which to form a chrysalis. You are warm and safe inside the chrysalis, but you are growing and changing. Finally, you must break out of the chrysalis. At first, your wings are wet and they are difficult to move. Then, as your wings dry, you begin to flap your wings until you finally fly away.

# Creative Movement *(cont.)*

## Streamer Stories *(cont.)*

### ❋ Waking Up

Pretend you are a very sleepy child who is just waking up for the day. As you open your eyes, you see the sunlight coming into your room. At first, it is too bright, but then you sense what a beautiful day it will be outside. You go outside to play. You run around with your friends doing your favorite activities. By the end of the day, you are very tired again. You go back inside and snuggle up to listen to a story before you fall asleep.

### ❋ A Tough Day

You have had a very tough day. Your feelings have been hurt and you are sad. As you come in the house from school, your mom notices that you are looking sad. She asks you what is wrong, and at first you do not want to talk about it. Then, mom bends down and gives you a hug. She tells you that we all have bad days and that she has a special treat for you. She goes to the refrigerator and pours you a glass of milk. Then, she goes to the cupboard and gets out two of your favorite cookies. After your snack, you feel better and go outside to play.

### ❋ The Chase

Pretend you are a fish swimming in the ocean. It is a beautiful day and you are swimming along looking for some food. Suddenly, a big shark comes into the area where you are swimming. At first you hide. But after a while, the shark spots you and begins to chase you. You swim and swim and swim, faster and faster and faster. Your heart is pumping. Finally, you find a cave in which you can swim, but the shark cannot. You go inside the cave. Once the shark goes away, you come out of the cave and go for a nice swim again.

### ❋ The Present

You have been counting the days until your birthday—five more days, four more days, three more days, two more days. Finally, it is the night before your birthday. You can hardly wait. You cannot get to sleep. Once you do get to sleep, you dream of all the fun you will have at your party. Finally, your special day is here. Everyone treats you like a queen or king. Your friends come for a party. You have fun playing games and eating cake, but the best part of the party is still to come—presents! You open each present. It is fun to unwrap the boxes, but the best part is when you can finally see the gift. Finally, you are done with your last gift. You don't remember getting a present from your mom and dad and you feel sad. But then, your dad comes out from the other room with a box. It is strange because the box is not wrapped and it has holes in it. When he bends down to show you the box, you see a puppy inside. You are so happy!

# Creative Movement *(cont.)*

## Part-To-Part

Have each student practice identifying body parts and movement by having him or her touch one body part to another body part. The commands can be very basic such as, "Touch your finger to your ankle," or use more complicated commands such as, "Touch your right elbow to your left knee." Use the directions below for ideas, or make up your own.

## Part-To-Part Activity Directions

- Touch your finger to your ear.
- Touch your wrist to your ankle.
- Touch one elbow to the other elbow.
- Touch your elbow to your toes.
- Touch your elbow to your hip.
- Touch your foot to your knee.
- Touch your knee to your ankle.

- Touch your right wrist to your left knee.
- Touch your left hand to your right shoulder.
- Touch your right knee to your left toes.
- Touch your right pinkie to your left ring finger.
- Touch your left thumb to your right ear.
- Touch your left ankle to your right knee.
- Touch your right hand to your left ear.

# Creative Movement *(cont.)*

## Materials:

- Actions Spinner (See below.)
- Feelings Spinner (See page 58.)

## I Feel. . .

Make the spinners that will be used in this game. Copy the spinner patterns on pages 57 and 58. Laminate the spinners for durability if possible. Attach the arrows with paper fasteners. Be sure to attach the paper fasteners loosely to laminated spinners and arrows to allow them to spin easily. Explain to each student that he or she will use creative movements to express feelings. Spin the Actions Spinner to indicate to the student the action that he or she will use. Spin the Feelings Spinner to indicate the way that the student will execute the action to show a feeling or mood. According to the indicators on the spinners, the student will walk, jump, or march in a silly, grumpy, angry, joyful, quiet, or excited way. You may want to review the feelings before beginning this activity.

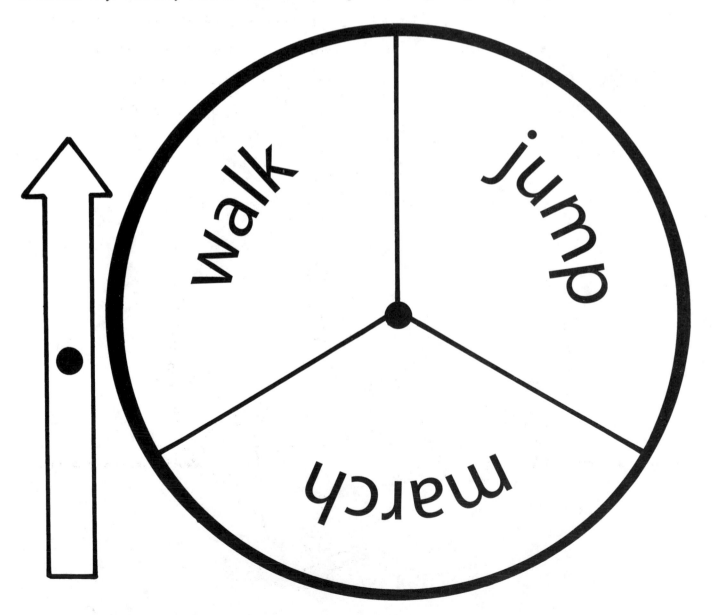

# Creative Movement *(cont.)*

**Feelings Spinner**

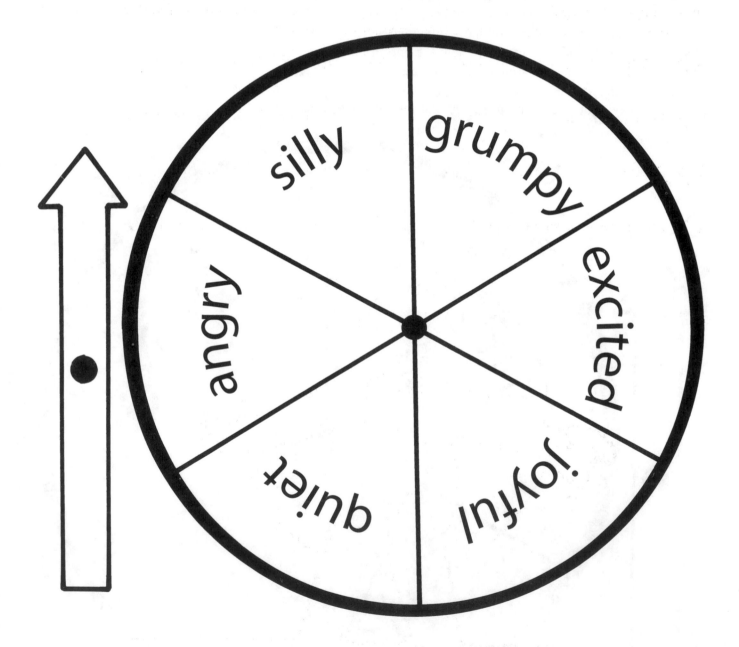

# Creative Movement *(cont.)*

## Materials:

- 1 beanbag per child (See pages 114–117 for beanbag patterns.)

## Over and Under

Give each child a beanbag. If beanbags are not available, almost any small manipulative will work, such as a small toy, a rectangular eraser, a pencil box, etc. Have the children use their beanbags as they follow simple one-step directions. (See below for ideas.) As they become skilled at following one-step directions, create more complicated one-step directions or two-step directions.

Put the beanbag under your foot.

Put the beanbag over your head.

Put the beanbag on your head.

Put the beanbag below your knees.

Put the beanbag above your shoulders.

Put the beanbag between your legs.

Put the beanbag under your chin.

Put the beanbag by your feet.

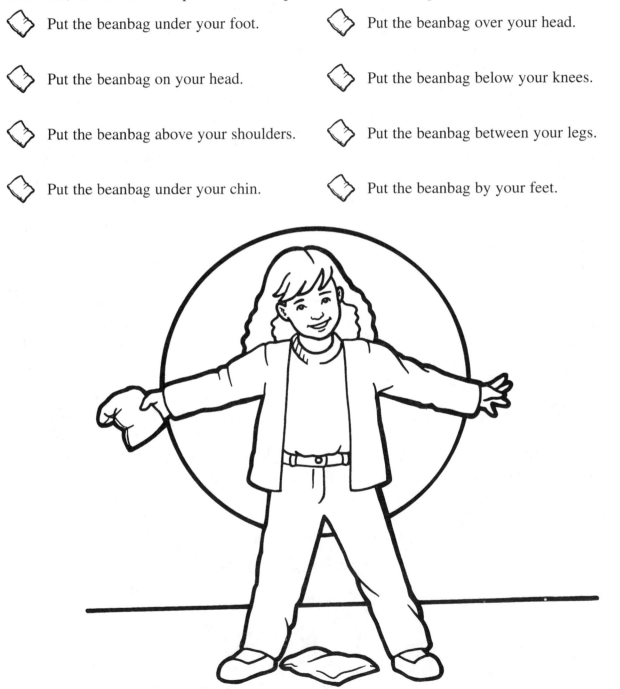

# Creative Movement *(cont.)*

## Materials:

- glow-in-the-dark stars
- a desk or table
- play dough
  (See pages 238–239 for recipes.)

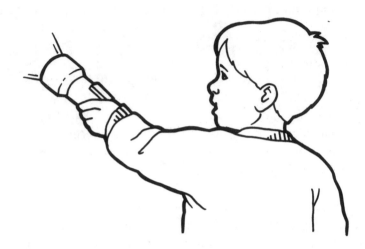

## Stars in the Sky

Have each student take a piece of play dough about the size of a grape, and roll it in his or her fingers until it is a ball.  Then, pick out one glow-in-the dark star, and put the ball of play dough on the back of it.  The student lies on his or her back and scoots under a table (the sky), reaches up and pushes the star on the bottom of the table.  (The play dough will make it stick.)  After he or she has stuck the star up in the "sky," have him or her scoot out from under the table using only his or her feet and arms.  Continue until each child has had a chance to place a star in the sky.  Depending on the size of the table, allow several students to lie on their backs and put their heads under the table.  Then, turn the classroom lights off, or down, for better visibility.

## Materials:

- flashlight (1 per student or group)

## Stars in the Sky II

Provide each student or each group of students with a flashlight.  Have each student lie on his or her back on the floor.  Then, turn the classroom lights off, or down, for better visibility.  The student can shine the flashlight on the ceiling in order to create stars.  A group of students can take turns.  Direct each student to do a variety of activities with his or her shining light.

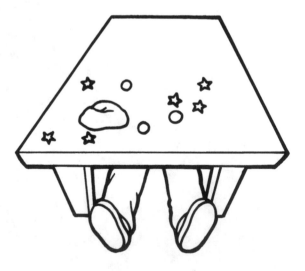

Use the light from the flashlight to:

- touch all four walls
- make small circles
- write letters or numbers

- touch all four corners of the room
- make large circles
- write a name

- draw a picture
- make swirls
- make lightning bolts

# Creative Movement *(cont.)*

## Materials:

- radio
- 10 tongue depressors
- a small cup

## Human Chain

Number the tongue depressors 1–10 and place them in a small cup so that they stand up. Explain to students that they will be moving around the room in time with the music. While the music is playing, the teacher selects a tongue depressor from the cup. When the number on the depressor is read, students must group themselves in chains by linking arms of students in numbers equal to the number called out. The chains of students continue moving to the rhythm of the music. "Extra" students can sit down on the side until the next number is called out, or continue to move to the music by themselves. Allow the students to complete the chains and move to the music in the chain for a minute or two before you choose another tongue depressor. As each depressor is selected, set it aside. This way the same number will not be called out twice until all the numbers are called. After all numbers have been called out, begin again.

# Creative Movement *(cont.)*

## Materials:

- chair or small step-stool (1 per child)

## Simon Says

Place a small step-step stool or chair in an area where the children can move around it easily. Then, play Simon Says. Give the children simple directions such as, "Simon says, walk around the chair. Simon says, sit down in the chair. Simon says, go behind the chair." Continue with directions, using the following directional words: over, under, by, next to, on, beneath, up, around, etc.

The children should only follow those directions that include Simon's name. If the directions do not include Simon's name, the children should not follow the directions (i.e., "Crawl under the desk"). Once the children are thoroughly familiar with how the game is played, let each child take a turn giving the directions.

## Variations

Set up a maze that will allow the children to crawl under a table, step up and over a chair, walk around a stand, go between two chairs, etc. To make the game more challenging, you can combine two directions. (For example, hop on one leg and crawl under the table, skip to the chair and then step up and over it.) Tell each child that if he or she successfully completes the maze, you will follow one of his or her mazes!

This game can also be played outdoors using locomotor movements such as walk, step, jump, hop, etc.

# Creative Movement *(cont.)*

## Materials:

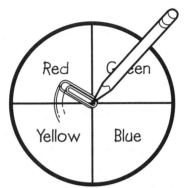

- construction paper in a variety of colors
- 2 spinners (See page 64.)
- a paper clip
- a pencil

## Color Board

Create your own board game. Cut circles 6" (15 cm) in diameter out of construction paper. You will want to have three circles each of red, yellow, blue, and green construction paper. Determine how you will arrange the colored circles on the ground. You may wish to design an organized pattern of three circles wide by four circles long, or you may choose to randomly scatter the circles. Secure the circles to the ground or carpet using tape or Velcro. Create spinners by copying the patterns on page 64. Use a pencil and paper clip to act as the spinner. Hold the pencil (at the eraser) with one hand and spin the paperclip, using the other hand.

Introduce this activity using only one student at a time on the circle patterns. You or the student spins both spinners. The first spinner determines which part of the body will be moved and the other spinner determines what color the body part will need to touch. The student can choose which circle he or she will touch, as long as it corresponds to the color that was spun. For very young students, you may wish to have them simply perform one movement. Once they have performed it, have them stand back up, then spin the spinners again. For older students, have them perform several movements at the same time. In this manner, students will practice moving their bodies around the game board in a variety of ways. Allow several students to play on the board game together. A student will have to carefully select which circle he or she will be moving to in order to avoid other children.

Create new spinners that require students to use their heads, elbows, knees, etc.

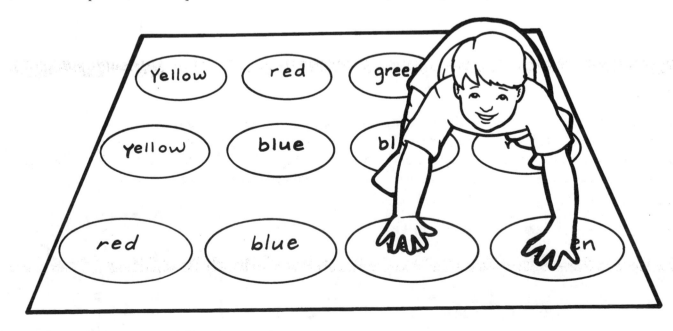

# Creative Movement *(cont.)*

**Spinners for Color Board**

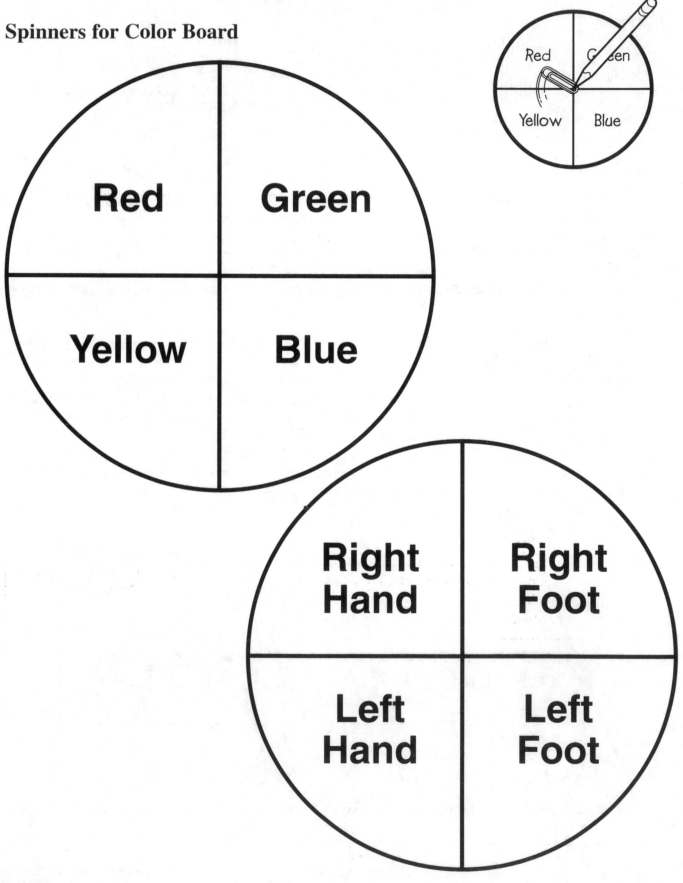

# Creative Movement *(cont.)*

## Materials:

• varies with the activity

## Rolling Activities

The movements below become progressively more difficult. Have each student complete some of the following rolling activities:

• Rock from side to side for 30–60 seconds while lying on his or her back, with arms on the floor over his or her head.

• Lie on the carpet and rub his or her body and extremities on it.

• Roll across the room any way he or she knows how.

• Roll across the room with arms over his or her head.

• Roll across the room with arms down at his or her side.

• Hold onto a ball and roll across the room with arms over his or her head.

• Roll over an object (another student, beanbag, etc.).

• Roll under an object (table, a sheet suspended over chairs, etc.).

• Roll between objects.

• Roll onto stomach, side, back, and reverse procedure.

• Roll to commands, such as "Stop" and "Go."

• Roll with a beanbag in hand, arms overhead, and then throw the beanbag at a target suspended 2' (61 cm) above the ground (wastebasket, dart board, target, etc.).

• Lie on the ground on his or her back and pretend to be an angel fluttering his or her wings (arm), then roll on his or her stomach and repeat.

• Roll with a beanbag between his or her knees.

• Roll "in" an object (boxes with ends cut out, tunnel, blanket, etc.).

• Lie on his or her stomach and hold onto ankles, rocking forward and backward.

# Creative Movement *(cont.)*

## Materials:

- varies with the activity

## Crawling Activities

The activities below are listed in order of difficulty. Have each student complete some of the following crawling activities.

- Lie on his or her stomach with hands under chin, lifting one leg at a time as high as possible (without rolling over on his or her side). First, lifting his or her legs separately, then together.

- Lie on his or her stomach and creep like a turtle, very slowly.

- Lie on his or her stomach and creep like a crocodile going after something to eat, very quickly.

- Lie on his or her stomach and crawl across the room, pivot on stomach, and return.

- Crawl on his or her stomach across the room backward (feet first).

- Spin around on his or her belly in a circle.

- Crawl up to a tape line on the floor and roll the rest of the way across the room.

- Crawl on a trail (zigzag, circle, square, etc.).

- Make a tunnel by bending at the waist and touching his or her hands on the floor; then another child crawls through the tunnel without touching the first child.

# Creative Movement *(cont.)*

## Materials:

- varies with the activity

## Creeping Activities

The activities in the list below become progressively more difficult. Have each student complete some of the following creeping activities:

- Spin around as quickly as possible in both directions, in a hands and knees position.

- Lie on his or her stomach and push up with the arms, while keeping knees on the ground.

- Lie on his or her back. The teacher names a body part and the child gently moves that part only (i.e., right pinkie, chin, foot, etc.).

- Find a body part while standing. For example, give directions for the student to put his or her elbows together, feet apart, touch one elbow, put knees together, etc.

- Creep with a washrag between his or her shoulder and chin, forward, backward, and sideways.

- Creep while pushing a ball across the room with only his or her head. If the child gets dizzy, encourge him or her to press his or her palms firmly on the ground until the dizziness passes.

- Get on hands and knees, lined up side by side (sets of two) with a tape line between them, keeping all fours on the floor, and trying to push the other child off balance without crossing the line.

- Get on hands and knees, move his or her head up and down, looking at the ceiling and then at the knees, keeping arms and legs firm.

- Get in pairs. Have each child lie on his or her back with knees bent and feet touching. See who can push the other over.

- Get on hands and knees, and lift one hand and balance for a count of 10. Repeat with the other hand and shake the hand all about. Then repeat with each leg.

# Creative Movement *(cont.)*

## Materials:

- varies with the activity

## Sitting Activities

The activities below are listed in order of difficulty. Have each student complete some of the following sitting activities:

- Sit in a cross-legged position. Have the child rotate his or her body from the waist in a circular motion, first with hands placed flat on the floor (for balance) and then without hands (arms folded over the head).

- Sit in a cross-legged position. Instruct the child to slump over forward, and then return to a straight sitting posture.

- Sit with legs straight out in front. Instruct the child to slump over forward, attempt to touch his or her head to knees and return to straight sitting posture.

- Lie on his or her back. Have the student raise his or her legs in the air to pump them in circles as on a bicycle.

- Sit with legs straight out in front. Instruct him or her to lie down and then sit up and curl into a tight ball.

- Sit in a cross-legged position. Have the child put his or her hands behind the neck and sway from side to side.

- Select a partner and stand back-to-back with elbows linked. From this position, he or she can attempt to sit down, and slowly try to stand up.

- Sit with legs straight out in front. Have the child place his or her hands on the floor at the sides of the hips. Pressing down, the student can straighten his or her arms until buttocks are off the floor and then hold there for a count of five.

- Sit with legs straight out in front. Have the child stretch to touch his or her right hand to left toes and left hand to right toes.

- Play musical chairs with chairs and stools of various heights so that the child must adjust accordingly.

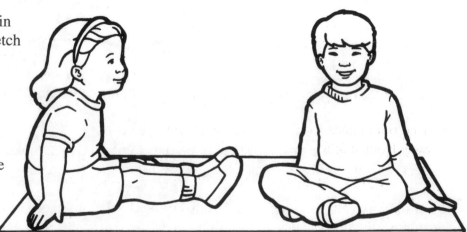

# Creative Movement (cont.)

## Materials:

- varies with the activity

## Kneeling Activities

The activities listed below are in order of difficulty. Have each student complete some of the following activities that can be done from a kneeling position:

- Kneel opposite from another child and take turns batting a ball, suspended from the ceiling, with one hand.

- Fold his or her arms and rock from side to side while kneeling.

- Fall forward onto his or her hands and return while kneeling.

- Select a partner and get in a kneeling position. Instruct each child to face the partner, hold hands, and rock forward, backward, and side-to-side.

- Face the wall in a kneeling position. With hands on the wall, he or she can "walk" sideways in both directions.

- Try to move forward, backward, and sideways while kneeling.

- Kick feet up and down while kneeling, with feet spread apart and then together (keeping knees together).

- Place his or her right foot down in front of the body and count to five. Repeat with the left leg.

- Kneel and sit on his or her heels with hands on the floor. He or she then leans forward, sliding the hands out in front of him or her until the chest touches the knees. In this position, he or she can swing arms to the left and then to the right.

- Hold both hands over his or her head and sway from side to side.

- Select a partner and get in a kneeling position. Each student "stands" shoulder to shoulder and tries to push the other off balance, using only his or her shoulders.

# Creative Movement *(cont.)*

## Materials:

• varies with the activity

## Standing Activities

The activities below are listed in order of difficulty. Have each student perform some of the following activities that can be done from a standing position:

• Stand independently, swinging one leg forward, backward, in and out, and in a circular motion. Repeat on the other leg.

• Keep his or her back against the wall. Have him or her slide the back up and down and rock side-to-side.

• Walk backward in and out of an obstacle course.

• Close his or her eyes and point to the ceiling, floor, teacher, etc.

• Lean against the wall, and roll across the wall.

• Face the wall, touching the wall with his or her nose, ear, forehead, etc.

• Stand with his or her back to the wall, and walk sideways along the wall.

• Rock on his or her feet, going from toes to heels. Repeat several times.

• Walk "small," then "tall" (squatting to tiptoes).

• Walk around the room with his or her side against the wall.

• Walk forward on a tape or chalk line. (Try backward, with crossover steps, and sideways.)

# Creative Movement *(cont.)*

## Materials:

- scooter board or skateboard (1 per child or group of children)
- hula hoop
- rope

## Scooter Board Activities

The activities below become progressively more difficult.  Have each student perform some of the following activities that can be done with a scooter board:

- Sit cross-legged on a scooter and propel himself or herself forward with his or her hands.  Have the student go in circles in both directions.

- Kneel on the scooter, spin around in circles, and then reverse.

- Sit or kneel on the scooter, move forwards, backwards, and then sideways.

- Sit cross-legged on the scooter, holding a hula hoop, while an adult pulls him or her.

- Lie on his or her stomach and scoot along the floor using only the feet.

- Kneel or sit on the scooter following various trails.

- Travel through an obstacle course using the scooter board.

- Lie on his or her stomach on the scooter board.  (Attach a rope to a door handle or the leg of a heavy desk.)  The student grabs the rope and pulls hard (using arms, not feet), hand over hand, to the end of the rope.

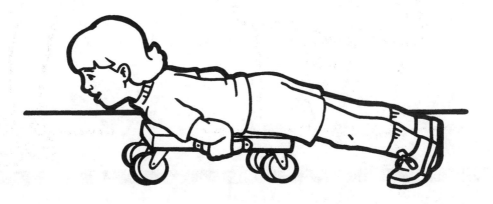

# Locomotor Skills

There are eight basic locomotor or traveling movements. Walk and run are self-explanatory. The following are definitions of the other movements. They are listed in the order of difficulty.

**Jump:** Take off on both feet and land on both feet.

**Hop:** Take off on one foot and land on the same foot.

**Leap:** Take off from one foot and land on the other foot. A leap is an extended running step.

**Gallop:** Perform a slide motion with the feet in a forward position. The feet need to be pointed in the same direction that the traveler is moving. The trailing leg is dragged behind as the traveler progresses forward.

**Skip:** This is a step/hop combination alternating the lead foot.

**Slide:** Step to the side and then close with the trailing foot. Body weight is then transferred to the trailing foot. The side of the body travels in the forward direction.

Development of basic locomotor skills is very important to a child's ability to gain further success in any other movement experience. A link between knowledge and skill enables the child to plan and use his or her skills more proficiently.

## Hints

♦ Hopping and jumping are the best locomotor movements to perform in a small space. There can be many repetitions without traveling a great distance.

♦ Many locomotor activities call for starting and stopping points. Markers to indicate these points are needed. Cones, coffee cans, or two-liter soda bottles filled with sand make good markers that are easily visible.

♦ Coffee can lids make great substitutes for the more expensive poly spots markers.

# Traveling

**Materials:**

- whistle, bell or other signaling device

## Walking Opposites

In this game, students walk in a predetermined way. At the signal, they have to walk the opposite way. You may need to spend some time reviewing opposites; introduce a few each day. Determine a signal which will indicate when students will do the opposite activity (e.g., a bell or a whistle).

Try some of the opposites listed below or make up some of your own.

| | |
|---|---|
| Walk on heels. | Walk on toes. |
| Walk quickly. | Walk slowly. |
| Walk forward. | Walk backward. |
| Walk left. | Walk right. |
| Walk standing tall. | Walk while slouched down. |
| Walk with arms in front. | Walk with arms behind your back. |
| Walk with arms behind you. | Walk with arms out in front of you. |
| Walk with hands on your head. | Walk with hands on your toes. |
| Walk with a partner. | Walk alone. |
| Walk a straight line. | Walk a curved line. |

Use some of these opposites while running, galloping, skipping, hopping, jumping, and sliding. Not all of the opposites will work with all of the locomotor movements, but try the ones that will.

# Traveling *(cont.)*

## Running Games

Children love to run, and it is an excellent gross motor activity. Pick a point on the playground to which you would like your students to run, or try some of these activities to spice up a period of time devoted to running.

Determine a signal that will identify when you want each student to change his or her movement. A whistle or a bell works well. The key is to have a signal that all students can hear.

## Materials:

- whistle, bell, or other signaling device

## Fast, Slow

Have each student run at a slow rate. When he or she hears the signal, have him or her run at a fast rate for a period of about 10–15 seconds. Signal again for the student to return to a slow rate. Continue signaling while he or she alternates between running quickly and slowly. Rather than having the students run, you can have them alternate between walking quickly and slowly.

## Freeze

Have each student run at a predetermined speed (fast, slow, medium, even a fast walk). When he or she hears the signal, the student must freeze. Use the signal to return the student to running.

## Lines

Define a large area in which students will be running. Remind each student to respect one another's personal space. Have the student run in a straight line. When he or she hears the signal, the student changes from running in a straight line to running in a circle. When the signal is sounded again, he or she returns to running in a straight line. Continue alternating straight lines and circles by signaling.

# Traveling *(cont.)*

## Running Games *(cont.)*

## Directions

Define an area in which play will take place. Have each student run in any direction. He or she should continue to run in that direction until hearing a signal (such as a whistle). When the student hears the signal, he or she turns and changes directions. (The student runs in the new direction until the signal is given again.) Continue in the same manner. This activity can be done by having each student freeze when he or she hears the signal.

Have each student practice running in a variety of ways:

| | |
|---|---|
| backward | sideways |
| quickly | slowly |
| lifting knees high | lifting knees low |
| to a destination | in place |
| in a straight line | in circles |
| while carrying nothing | while carrying a beanbag or ball |

Combine running with a variety of other activities. Determine an activity you would like each student to do. (Select an activity from below or determine your own.) Explain that when he or she hears the signal, the student should begin running. When he or she hears the signal again, the student stops and performs the activity. When the signal is given again, the student resumes running.

| | |
|---|---|
| jumping jacks | toe-touches |
| sit-ups | push-ups |
| knee bends | windmills (hand touches opposite foot) |
| hop | jump |
| make a face | touch the ground, then stomach, then reach for the sky |

## Everyone Is It

In this version of tag, everyone is it. Each student attempts to tag one another. If a student is tagged, he or she must sit down on the ground until the next game.

## Bandage Tag

This is another version of Everyone Is It. However, when a student is tagged, he or she must hold that area of his or her body with one hand. The student can get tagged and hold two areas of his or her body (one for each hand) before he or she is out.

# Traveling *(cont.)*

## Materials:

• Animal Action Cards (See pages 77–78.)

## Going Ape

Copy the Animal Action Cards. Cut the cards apart and laminate them for durability.

Tell the students that they are going to have to use their imaginations in order to act like animals. Place the cards facedown on a table. Select a card and read it to the children. Have students pretend to be the animal that is on the card. You may wish to read only the action first. Then, once students are involved with acting out the animal, ask them to make the noise that corresponds to that animal. Suggestions for activities and noises are listed on the cards, as appropriate. Repeat until all of the animals have been acted out. Challenge students to think of their own animals to imitate.

An alternative to this activity is to have one student select a card and pretend to be the animal. The student that is acting cannot make any sounds. The rest of the children must guess what animal is being imitated.

## Materials:

• Walking Action Cards (See page 79.)

## Walk Like This

Copy the Walking Action Cards. Cut the cards apart and laminate them for durability.

Each Walking Action Card provides a unique and fun way for students to practice movement around the classroom or playground. Place the Walking Action Cards facedown on a table. Begin by having the students walk in a circle around the classroom. Then, select a card from the stack and read it to the students. Have them walk in the manner described on the card. Repeat until all of the cards have been acted out.

# Traveling *(cont.)*

## Animal Action Cards

**Bear**

Pretend you are a bear by walking on all fours. Then, growl using a deep voice.

**GROWL!**

**Elephant**

Pretend you are an elephant walking around the ring at the circus. Join your arms in front of you. Sway your arms like a trunk. Parade around the room.

**SWAY!**

**Lion**

Pretend you are a lion. Walk on all fours and then roar.

**ROAR!**

**Worm**

Pretend you are a worm. Wiggle on the floor.

**WIGGLE!**

**Frog**

Pretend you are a frog. See how many different ways you can jump.

**JUMP!**

**Dinosaur**

Pretend you are a dinosaur. Stomp around the room like a dinosaur. Imagine what kind of noise a dinosaur would make, and make that noise.

**STOMP!**

# Traveling *(cont.)*

## Animal Action Cards *(cont.)*

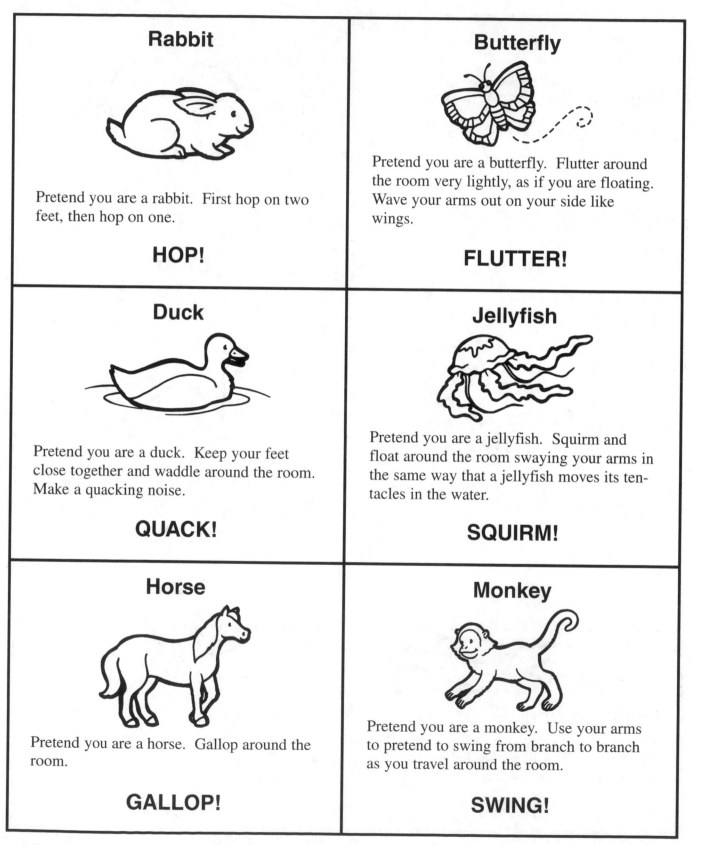

**Rabbit**

Pretend you are a rabbit. First hop on two feet, then hop on one.

**HOP!**

**Butterfly**

Pretend you are a butterfly. Flutter around the room very lightly, as if you are floating. Wave your arms out on your side like wings.

**FLUTTER!**

**Duck**

Pretend you are a duck. Keep your feet close together and waddle around the room. Make a quacking noise.

**QUACK!**

**Jellyfish**

Pretend you are a jellyfish. Squirm and float around the room swaying your arms in the same way that a jellyfish moves its tentacles in the water.

**SQUIRM!**

**Horse**

Pretend you are a horse. Gallop around the room.

**GALLOP!**

**Monkey**

Pretend you are a monkey. Use your arms to pretend to swing from branch to branch as you travel around the room.

**SWING!**

# Traveling *(cont.)*

**Walking Action Cards**

| | |
|---|---|
| Walk as though the room is full of something gooey. | Walk around the room as if you were on a balance beam. Follow a line on the floor or a piece of tape. |
| Walk on your tiptoes. | Walk around the room on the heels of your feet. |
| Walk over to a friend and whisper something in his or her ear. | Walk as if you were walking up a hill. |
| Walk around the room like a king or queen. | Walk around the room in a zigzag line. |

# Traveling *(cont.)*

## Materials:

- sheets of newspaper (2 per student)
- chalk

## Newspaper Walk

Use chalk to mark off points for students to begin and end. Give each child two sheets of newspaper. A student begins at the starting line. While the student is proceeding to the ending line, he or she may move only by stepping on his or her sheets of newspaper. A student may step on one paper, lay the other one down and step on it, turn and pick up the one he or she just stepped off and drop it down for the next step, etc. This activity may be used to have students practice jumping and hopping, too.

# Traveling *(cont.)*

## Materials:

- none

## Parts

Arrange to play this game in a large, unobstructed area. Have students scatter throughout the play area. Select a motor skill that you would like the students to practice.

The activity begins when the teacher calls out the phrase, "parts to parts." Each student begins moving, using agreed upon locomotor movements such as running, walking, skipping, sliding, galloping, hopping, jumping, "animal walking," etc. When a leader calls out "part to part" again, the students pair up and freeze. The leader calls out a particular body part, e.g., toes. Student partners stand with the chosen body parts touching each other (e.g., students stand facing each other with the toes of the left feet touching). The leader calls out one or two other body parts for students to touch before calling out "part to part." The leader then calls out a new locomotor movement for students to do. When the leader calls out "part to part" again, partners freeze and more body parts are called for students to touch with their partners.

## Variation

Call out words that rhyme with the body part that you want students to touch, such as "sack to sack" instead of "back to back" so students have to figure out what body parts they are supposed to touch. You may use nonsense words that rhyme, such as "nelbow to nelbow," so that students have to figure out that they are to touch elbows.

# Traveling *(cont.)*

## Materials:

- beanbag (1 per child)

## Beanbag Movement

Provide each child with a beanbag. Be sure to allow time for the student to experiment with the beanbag before you ask him or her to listen to directions. Ask the student to try some of the following movements with the beanbag:

 Place the beanbag on your head and walk around the room.

 Place the beanbag on your back and crawl around the room.

 Place the beanbag on your foot and walk around the room.

 Place the beanbag between your legs and jump around the room like a kangaroo.

 Place the beanbag on your shoulder and walk backward around the room.

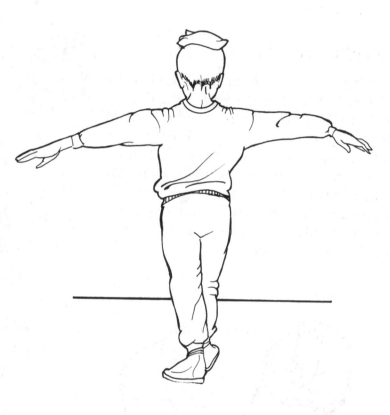

## Variation

Divide the class into teams. Have each team race against other teams in a relay. Walk to a determined point in the room (or outside). Then, call out movements for the students to do. For example, the first time it is a student's turn, have him or her walk (from the predetermined point) with the beanbag on his or her head to another finishing point. Once each student on the team has completed that activity, have him or her place the beanbag on his or her foot. The first team to have all of its members complete the activities is the winner.

# Traveling *(cont.)*

## Materials:

- chalk or masking tape

Once students become skilled at wheelbarrow walking, crab walking, or chimp walking, create lines for the students to walk along. Vary the lines so that they are straight, wavy, and zig-zagged. The children can also have individual or team races in these positions, or even play soccer!

## Wheelbarrow Walk

Have one student get down on his or her hands and knees. A partner will pick up the first child's legs and rest them on his or her hips. (Depending on the age of your children, they may need to be held at the knees or ankles. The younger the child, the less arm strength he or she will have, thus, needing to be held at the knees for more support.) The student on his or her hands tries to move forward using only the hands and arms.

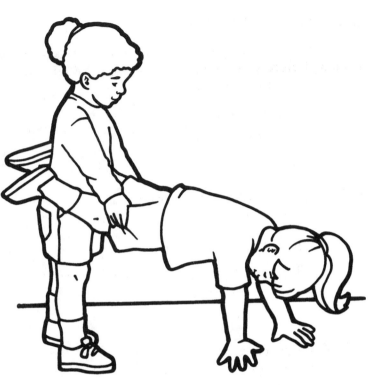

## Crab Walk

Have each child practice walking like a crab, along the ground with both feet and both hands on the ground.

## Chimp Walk

Direct each child to walk like a chimp by spreading his or her feet apart, bending over, and grabbing the ankles.

# Traveling *(cont.)*

## Materials:

- none

## Mother, May I?

Have the children stand side-by-side on one side of the room, facing the teacher who is on the other side of the room. The teacher acts out the role of "mother," naming a child and giving a direction such as, "Mary, take two baby steps forward." The named child responds with, "Mother (or Father), may I?" The teacher then answers, "Yes, you may." If the child forgets to ask for permission, he or she must go back to the starting place. Play continues until one child reaches the teacher's position. He or she then becomes the mother or father, and the remaining children return to their starting positions across the room. Vary the directions for each child by changing the kind of movement and/or the number of moves.

Use some of the following directions:

- Take (number) baby steps.

- Take (number) jumps.

- Take (number) giant steps.

- Take (number) hops.

- Skip (number) times.

- Twirl around (number) times.

As the child becomes more proficient, combine two or more directions. For an older child, you may vary the script as follows:

"Mary, take two baby steps forward."

"Mother, may I?"

"No, you may not. Take three hops forward."

"Mother, may I?"

"Yes, you may."

Or, "Mary, take two baby steps and one hop forward."

# Traveling *(cont.)*

## Materials:

- masking tape (4" or 10 cm wide)
- beanbag (1 per child)

## Walk the Line

Make two lines on the floor or carpet using masking tape. Make each line the same length (approximately 8' [2.4 m] and about 2' [61 cm] apart). These lines will be your "train track." Using the train track lines, each student can complete some of the activities below:

- Walk along one of the tape lines by putting one foot in front of the other. Continue until you get to the end of the line.

- Make engine movements when walking on one line by placing the right foot in front of the left, moving it forward about 5" (13 cm) and bringing the left foot up to bump the right foot. Continue until you get to the end of the track.

- Cross feet over while walking on the line, so the right foot crosses to the left of the line and the left foot crosses to the right of the line. Have the student continue crossing to the end of the line.

- Jump with two feet at the same time on the lines—right foot on the right line and left foot on the left line.

- Walk along the lines on all fours by bending over in order to place the left hand and foot on the left line and the right hand and foot on the right line.

## Variation

Once a student has practiced and has become skilled at walking the line in any of the ways above, challenge him or her to complete the same activities with a beanbag balanced on the top of his or her head. In addition, you can provide two beanbags and have the child balance the beanbags on the top of his or her shoes while performing the activity.

# Traveling *(cont.)*

## Materials:

- stilts (1 pair per group)

## Stilts

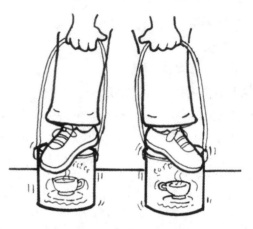

Stilts are an excellent way for students to practice movement activities. Stilts are commercially available; however, it is easy to make a pair, too. (See the directions at the bottom of the page.) Allow students some experimental time to become accustomed to walking on stilts. Then have each student try some of the stilts activities below:

- Walk on the stilts while holding both ropes in one hand.

- Stay on a line, created by chalk or masking tape, while walking on the stilts.

- Jump while on the stilts.

- Practice stepping up on a small step stool. Be sure that the step is not too high, and that he or she will be able to manage it while on stilts.

- Make several pairs of stilts and let students have "giant" relay races. Determine a beginning and ending point and conduct the races. You may want to hold the races on the grass.

- Create an obstacle course for each student to go through on the stilts. Use objects which he or she will be able to navigate through safely while on stilts.

---

## Materials:

- 2 small coffee cans
- rope

### Directions for Making a Pair of Stilts

Punch two holes across from each other in the bottom of each metal juice can or coffee can (the end without the opening). Thread a rope or twine through the holes, securing each end with a knot, leaving the ends long enough for the student to hold onto when standing on the cans. Flip the cans over and have the child stand on them, holding the rope ends.

---

# Jumping and Hopping

## Materials:

- newspaper sheets
- black marker
- tape

## Newspaper Jump

Place 7–10 newspaper sheets on the floor within jumping distance. Tape them down. Write a number on each newspaper. The numbers can be in sequential or random order. A student begins by standing just in front of the newspaper numbered 1. He or she takes a turn jumping from 1 to 2, all the way to the highest number. Then, the student jumps on all the odd numbers, or all the even numbers. For example, go from 2 to 4, or 3 to 5, etc.

Have the student try jumping, hopping, jumping sideways, or jumping backward.

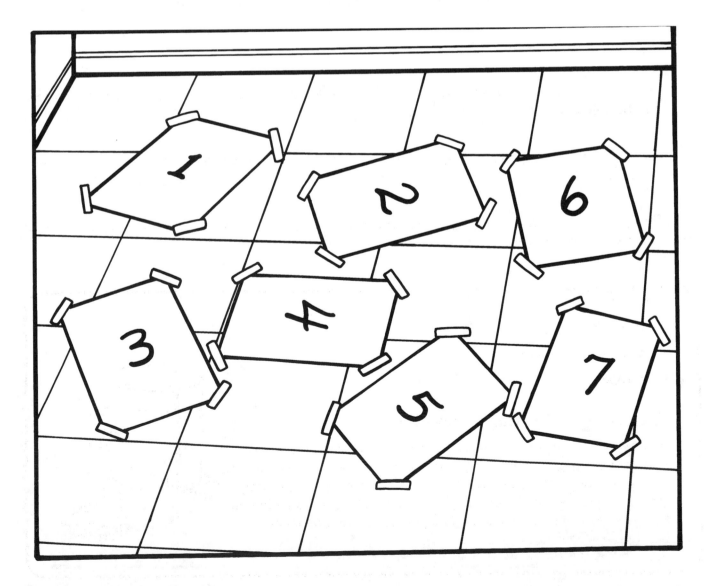

# Jumping and Hopping *(cont.)*

## Materials:

- masking tape or a jump rope
- beanbag

## Line Jump

Create a straight line on the ground using a piece of masking tape or rope. Determine the length based on the abilities of your children.

Have each student try each of the following activities:

- Practice jumping on the line.
- Jump while holding a beanbag.
- Toss the beanbag in front of himself or herself, trying to have it land on the line. The student jumps on the line until the beanbag is reached. Once the beanbag is picked up, he or she tosses it toward the line again.
- Practice jumping next to the line.
- Practice jumping backward, next to the line.

Have the student repeat the activities above on a curved or zig-zag line (created by the teacher). The activities can be used while walking and hopping, too.

# Jumping and Hopping *(cont.)*

## Materials:

- masking tape
- cardboard boxes
- chairs

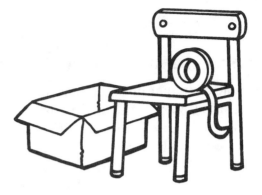

## Jumping Obstacle Course

Create an obstacle course through which your students can jump. Each of the activities should be appropriately designed for students to jump. Consider some of the options below, then set up a course based on the space and materials you have available. Use the obstacle course to have each student practice directional words:

### On

Create a line, either straight or curved, with masking tape. The student must jump along the line.

### Over

Set cardboard boxes in the obstacle course for each student to jump over. Be sure the boxes are an appropriate height for the jumping abilities of your students.

### Around

Set up chairs or any other appropriate object for the student to jump around.

### Through

Have the obstacle course go through a doorway.

### Under

Hang an object, such as a two-sided decoration, from the ceiling. Route the obstacle course so that the student has to jump under the decoration.

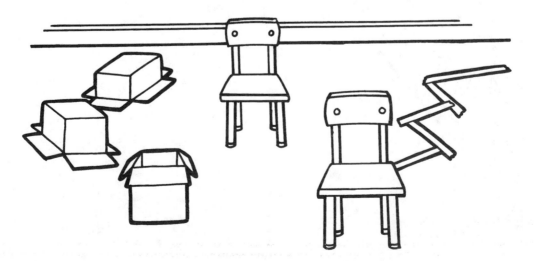

# Jumping and Hopping *(cont.)*

## Materials:

- Footprint Patterns (See page 91.)
- rope or masking tape

## Three-Jump Obstacle Course

Create a straight line with masking tape, or by laying a rope on the ground. Copy nine sets of footprints onto cardstock and tape them down as follows: three footprints on the left side of the line, three on the right side of the line, and three more on the left side of the line (see diagram). A student jumps, with two feet together, on the three sets of footprints on the left side of the line. Then, he or she jumps, with two feet together, on the right side of the line. Finally, the student jumps, with two feet together, on the three sets of footprints on the left side of the line.

# Jumping and Hopping *(cont.)*

**Footprint Patterns**

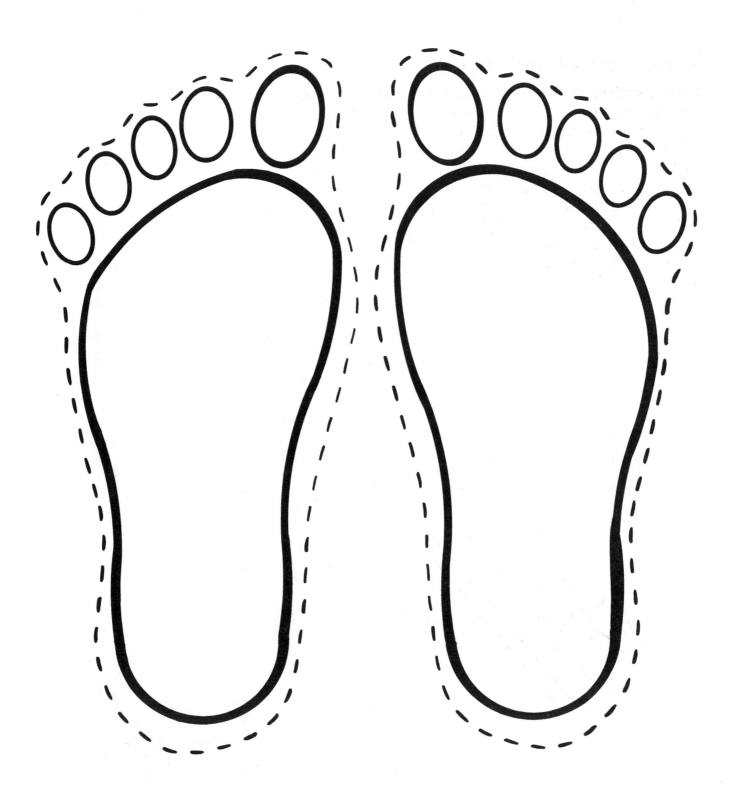

# Jumping and Hopping *(cont.)*

## Materials:

- Footprint Patterns (See page 91.)
- rope or masking tape

## Hopping on Alternating Feet

Create a straight line with masking tape, or by laying a rope on the ground. Copy nine sets of footprints onto cardstock. Cut the footprints apart so that you have patterns of left feet and right feet. Select a pattern from the options below, and tape the footprints down. A student hops on each footprint with the corresponding foot. For example, when he or she sees a right footprint, the student hops with only the right foot on that pattern. You can create patterns of your own, or have the children help you.

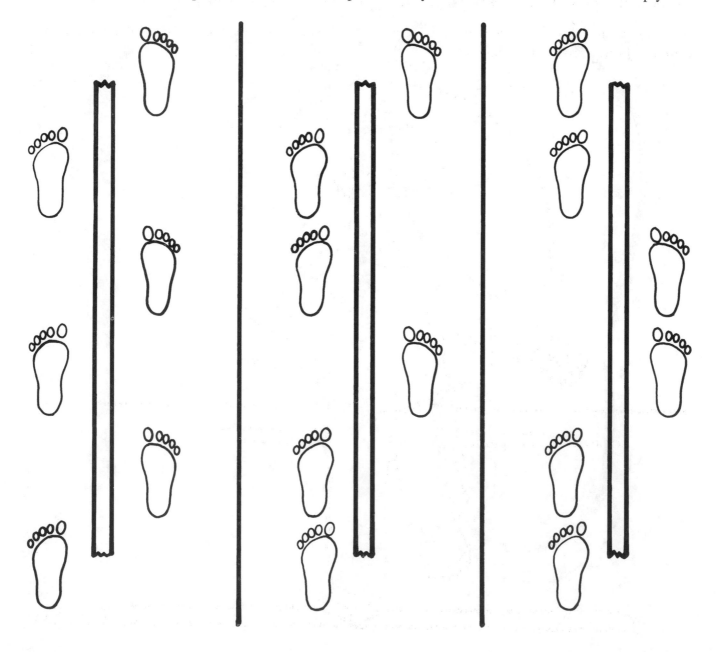

# Jumping and Hopping *(cont.)*

**Materials:**

- chalk

## Hop, Skip, and Jump!

In a clear, safe area, mark a starting and finishing line with chalk. (Six yards or five meters apart will be a good distance.) Time each child as he or she hops on one foot at a time from start to finish. Then time him or her skipping, keeping in mind that skipping is often difficult for young children. Finally, time the child jumping from one foot to both, or both to both. Tell each child which way he or she was quickest and see if he or she can beat the score on a second trial. Remember, the emphasis is on having fun, practicing movement skills, and trying to beat each child's own score. If the activity becomes too competitive, stop keeping times and focus on practicing locomotor skills.

In addition, this activity can be completed with another locomotor movement. Try walking, running, leaping, sliding, crawling, rolling, etc.

# Skipping

Skipping is often one of the most difficult locomotor skills for students to learn. For a child who is having difficulty skipping, provide a lot of jumping and hopping practice first. Then, combine hopping on the right and left foot.

### To Skip:

Hop on right

Hop on left

*Repeat*

Then speed it up.

Once the student has the idea, you will probably see him or her skipping everywhere! Then, try some of the activities below:

Teach the students the skipping song, "Skip To My Lou."

## Skip to My Lou

Skip, skip, skip to my Lou,

Skip, skip, skip to my Lou,

Skip, skip, skip to my Lou,

Skip to my Lou my darling.

Fly's in the buttermilk, shoo fly, shoo.

Fly's in the buttermilk, shoo fly, shoo.

Fly's in the buttermilk, shoo fly, shoo.

Skip to my Lou my darling.

## Materials:

- beanbags

## Beanbag Touch

Scatter beanbags on the ground all around the area you will be using. A student skips around in the area until he or she hears a signal (whistle). When the student hears the signal, he or she runs to touch as many beanbags as possible before hearing the signal again (have each student count how many beanbags he or she touched). Give each student approximately five seconds to run around touching beanbags. Upon the next signal, have the student resume skipping. Continue for four or five rounds.

# Galloping

## Materials:

- Barn Pattern (See page 96.)
- markers

## Horses

In this activity, each student pretends he or she is a horse. Make a copy of the Barn Pattern for each child. Color the pattern, or copy it onto brown or red paper. Spread the patterns out on the ground in the area you will be playing. Secure each pattern to the floor with tape or Velcro™. If you laminate the patterns for durability, be sure the patterns are very secure to avoid injury. Each child begins on a Barn Pattern. At a signal, the child begins galloping like a horse within the designated play area. When he or she hears the signal again, the student gallops back to the barn. Once the student reaches the barn, he or she simply stands on it. Signal again to let the student know he or she can gallop around freely. Continue in the same manner.

This activity can be done with other locomotor movements. For example, each child can be a bunny while practicing hopping, or a kangaroo while jumping. Create your own versions of this activity. Also, you can use a beanbag or a hula hoop in place of the Barn Pattern.

# Galloping *(cont.)*

## Barn Pattern

# Combined Locomotor Skills

## Materials:

- Locomotor Movement Cards (See pages 98–102.)

## From Here to There

Make Locomotor Movement Cards (see directions below). Arrange the cards in a large circle. Divide the students according to how many Locomotor Movement Cards you will be using, and place one group of students next to each card. Determine the direction in which students will be rotating. Each student performs the activity on the card as he or she rotates from card to card. For example, if a student begins at a card labeled "Jump," the student must jump while rotating to the next card. When the student gets to the next card, he or she performs the activity listed on the card while rotating to the following card. Rotate students for a determined amount of time or until they have had a chance to perform all of the motions.

You can make more Locomotor Movement Cards using the Animal Action Cards on pages 77–78. Follow the instructions below for making the cards. When using the animal movements for this activity it helps if students are already familiar with each action.

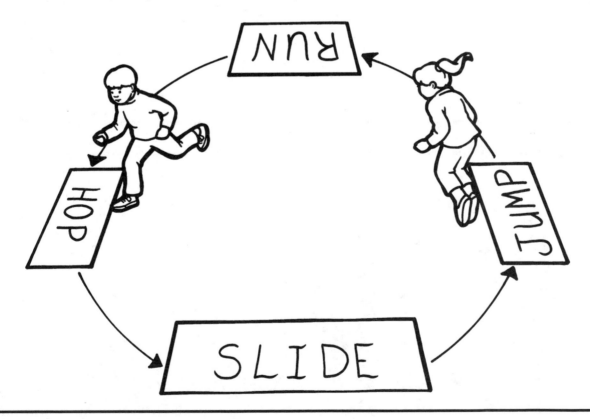

## Directions for Making Locomotor Movement Cards

Make Movement Cards (see pages 98–102) by copying the pages onto transparency film. Project the transparency onto a piece of tagboard. Trace the images onto the tagboard with a permanent marker. Color and laminate if desired.

# Combined Locomotor Skills *(cont.)*

## Locomotor Movement Cards

# Combined Locomotor Skills (cont.)

**Locomotor Movement Cards** *(cont.)*

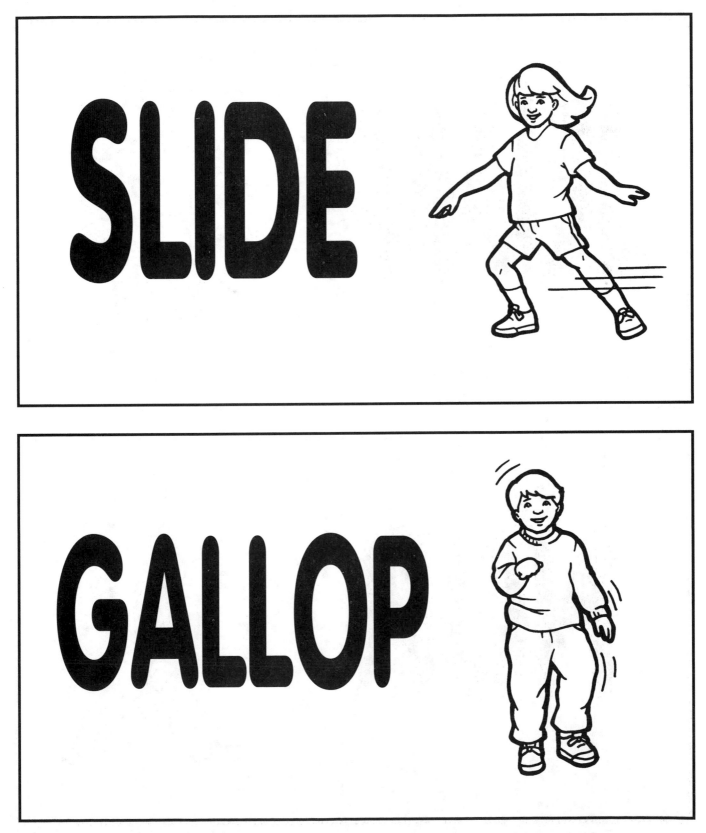

SLIDE

GALLOP

# Combined Locomotor Skills (cont.)

## Locomotor Movement Cards (cont.)

# Combined Locomotor Skills *(cont.)*

**Locomotor Movement Cards** *(cont.)*

# Combined Locomotor Skills (cont.)

## Locomotor Movement Cards (cont.)

WHEELBARROW WALK

CHIMP WALK

# Ball Skills

*Manipulative skills* such as throwing, catching, rolling, bouncing, and hitting involve the use of many body parts to propel and receive an object. Children enjoy the challenging play opportunities that can be created by using balls.

Throwing, catching, rolling, bouncing, and hitting help develop judgment and decision-making skills. Students must decide such issues as "In what direction should I throw?" and "How much force should I use?" when propelling an object. Students use information transmitted through the sense organs to make judgments about their environment. Eye-muscle training and the development of hand/eye coordination are very important in developing other useful life skills, such as keyboarding and driving.

**Hints:**

Beach balls are very light and inexpensive and do not threaten children who have not developed the judgment skills needed to catch harder, heavier balls.

Large sponges, purchased in quantity from the discount store, and wadded paper make good alternatives to balls used in throwing games. They won't break items in the classroom and they don't travel far when thrown.

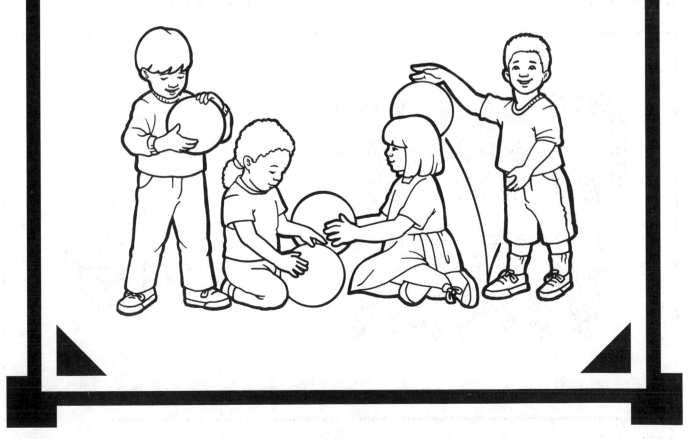

# Throwing and Catching

## Materials:

- scarf or 12" (30 cm) square of fabric or facial tissue (1 per student)

## Scarf Toss

Using scarves is an excellent and non-threatening way to introduce catching skills to students. The scarf moves slowly, providing the student many opportunities to catch it as it falls.

To start, give each child one scarf. A student tosses the scarf up in the air using his or her arms and wrists. As the scarf floats back down toward the ground, the student tries to catch the scarf with his or her hands. In the beginning, the student can catch the scarf with both hands. Then, as he or she becomes more familiar with how the scarf will fall and how to go about catching it, he or she can try to catch it using only one hand.

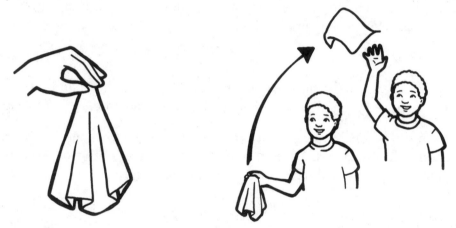

Once the student has the idea of how to catch the falling scarf, challenge him or her with some of the activities below:

- Toss the scarf up in the air with the right hand and catch it with the right hand.

- Toss the scarf up in the air with the left hand and catch it with the left hand.

- Toss the scarf up in the air with the right hand and catch it with the left hand.

- Toss the scarf up in the air with the left hand and catch it with the right hand.

- Toss the scarf up in the air and clap once before catching it.

- Toss the scarf up in the air and touch your toes before catching it.

- Toss the scarf, releasing it when the arm is above the head.

- Toss the scarf. Catch the scarf at waist level.

- Toss the scarf. Catch the scarf while it is still overhead.

- Toss the scarf over your right shoulder. Turn around and catch the scarf with the right hand.

- Toss the scarf over your left shoulder. Turn around and catch the scarf with the left hand.

★ Most of these activities can be completed with a beanbag, too!

# Throwing and Catching *(cont.)*

## Materials:

- scarf or 12" (30 cm) square of fabric or facial tissue (1 per pair)
- beanbag (1 per pair)
- ball (1 per pair)

## Partner Toss

Have pairs of students face each other standing toe-to-toe. One student tosses the scarf, and the other student catches it. Once both students have successfully tossed and caught the scarf, have each child take a step backward. Continue having the children take one step backward after each successful toss and catch by the pair.

Have each pair of children stand about 3' (91 cm) apart facing each other. Call out commands for the students to follow when throwing or catching the scarf. For example, "Only use your right hand."

- Only use your left hand.

- Jump once before tossing the scarf.

- Jump once before catching the scarf.

- See page 104 for additional ideas of ways partners can toss and catch the scarf.

## Variation

Have the children repeat some of the activities listed above using a a beanbag or ball.

# Throwing and Catching *(cont.)*

## Materials:

- scarves or 12" (30 cm) squares of fabric in 3 different colors (1 set per child)

## Scarf Juggling

Give each child a set of three scarves. Teach him or her how to hold the scarf in the center, extend the arm over the head and toss it in the air, and then catch the scarf at waist level as it floats down.

## Two Scarf Juggling

Begin teaching juggling by only using two scarves (for example red and white). Have each child begin with the red scarf in the right hand and the white scarf in the left hand. He or she tosses the red scarf up in the air. While the red is up in the air, the student transfers the white scarf from the left hand to the right hand. Then, the student catches the red scarf with the left hand. Repeat, this time tossing the white scarf in the air and transferring the red scarf. Once the student has practiced for a while, give verbal cues (call out a color or say "toss") in order for him or her to get faster at tossing and catching the scarves. As the student becomes skilled at tossing and transferring two scarves, have him or her try juggling with three scarves.

## Three Scarf Juggling

The movements will be similar to Two Scarf Juggling, just a little faster. In order to juggle three scarves (for example red, white, and blue), have each child begin with the red scarf in the right hand and the white and blue scarves in the left hand. He or she tosses the red scarf in the air. As the red scarf is being tossed, the child transfers the blue scarf to the right hand and begins to toss it. Then as the red scarf is floating down, he or she transfers the white scarf from the left hand to the right hand and catches the red scarf with the left hand. Using scarves really slows these movements down, since it takes a while for the scarves to float down. The student usually catches on quickly once he or she gets the idea that one scarf will always be in the air, one scarf is being caught, and one scarf is being tossed.

# Throwing and Catching *(cont.)*

## Materials:

- newspaper ball (1 per child)

## Catch Practice

A piece of newspaper, wadded up in a ball, works well to provide students practice in catching. The newspaper ball has the shape of a ball, but does not have the force of a real ball. Have each student practice throwing and catching a newspaper ball with the activities below:

- Toss the ball up in the air, then catch it with two hands.

- Toss the ball up in the air, then catch it with the right hand.

- Toss the ball up in the air, then catch it with the left hand.

- Stand toe-to-toe with a partner. Toss the ball back and forth from partner to partner. After each successful throw and catch by both partners, have the pair take one step back. At the point which a student does not catch the ball, both partners take a step toward each other. The pair continues to practice throwing and catching the ball until each student catches the ball and can step backward again.

- Have partners stand facing each other at about 3' (90 cm) apart. A student lifts one leg to practice throwing the ball under his or her knee.

- Partners stand about 3' (90 cm) apart. Have one partner turn around. A student practices throwing the ball through his or her legs.

- Partners stand about 3' (90 cm) apart. Have one partner turn around. A student practices throwing the ball over his or her shoulder.

- Practice these same activities using a beanbag. When students become more skilled at catching and throwing the newspaper ball or beanbag, use a real ball.

# Throwing and Catching *(cont.)*

## Materials:

- a ball of yarn

## Weaving a Web

Arrange the students in a circle. (Students can either sit or stand for this activity.) Give one student a ball of yarn. Demonstrate how to hold onto the end of the yarn with one hand, and toss the ball of yarn with the other hand. Each time a student catches the ball, he or she must take hold of a piece of the yarn before tossing the ball to anther student. The student continues to hold the yarn as the ball passes to other students. The ball of yarn is tossed from student to student in a random fashion until each student has had the yarn. The result is a web.

### ❀ First Day of School

Try this activity on the first day of school. Provide a question for each student to answer when he or she catches the yarn. For example, the first time you do it, each student may say his or her name. Repeat the activity and have each student tell what he or she did on summer vacation, or what he or she wants to learn this school year.

### ❀ Halloween Fun

Use black yarn and do this activity at Halloween. Have students sit on the floor in a circle. Once the web has been spun, have each child carefully set down the part of the yarn that he or she is holding (keeping the web intact). Provide a plastic spider for each student to place on the web. Students can sit around the web while eating a snack, or while telling scary stories.

### ❀ Units of Study

Use the web activity as a way to get all students involved in the topic you are currently studying. Use it before you begin a new unit, while filling out a KWL (what you *know*, what you *want to know*, and what you *learned*) chart. Or, use the activity during or after a unit of study and have each child tell you what he or she learned, or his or her favorite part of the unit. Using this technique requires that every student contributes eventually.

# Throwing and Catching *(cont.)*

## Materials:

- balls of yarn in different colors

## Stardom!

Children will love creating a big, soft, fuzzy star while they practice throwing and catching skills. Arrange students in groups of five, according to the diagram below. Number each student in the group (1–5) and have him or her face inward. (It may be helpful to tape the number to each child to help him or her keep track.) It is hepful to have arrows taped to the floor or carpet. Begin with #1 and have that child hold one end of the yarn while tossing the yarn to #2, across to #3, over to #4, across to #5, and back to #1. Rotate the lines. Repeat with different colors of yarn.

**Variation:** Have children call out the names of things that are the color of the yarn being tossed.

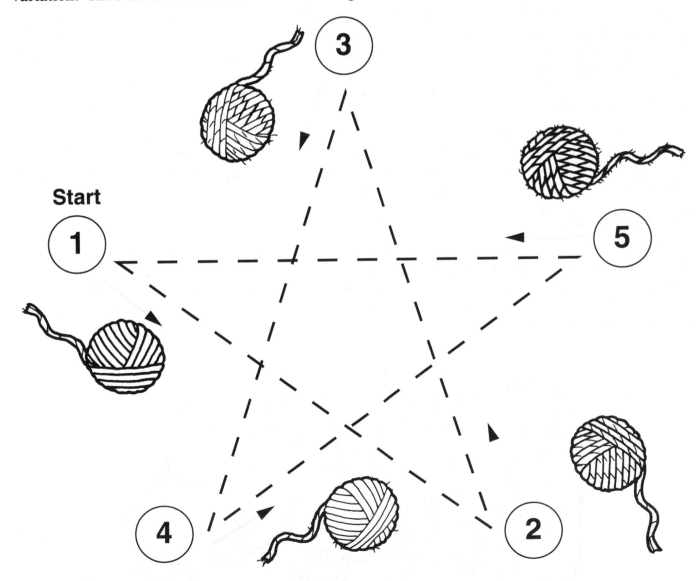

**Teacher Note:** Have a camera ready when the star is finished!

# Throwing and Catching *(cont.)*

## Materials:

- a beach ball
- a permanent marker

## Word Ball

In this activity, students throw and catch a beach ball while practicing some basic skills. Determine a skill that you would like students to practice. Label a beach ball with words, letters, or numbers based on the skill (write on the ball with a permanent marker). Have the students stand in a circle. Explain to each student that he or she will throw the ball to another student who will catch the ball. The students continue to throw and catch the ball until they hear a signal. The student who has the ball at the signal will read the word, letter, or number written on the ball that is closest to his or her right thumb. He or she then gives an answer that corresponds to the skill being practiced. For example, a beach ball can be programmed with words. When a signal is given, the student who has the ball must generate a word that rhymes with the word closest to his or her right thumb.

Consider programming beach balls for students to practice:

- letter identification
- letter sounds
- addition facts
- subtraction facts
- sight words
- rhyming words

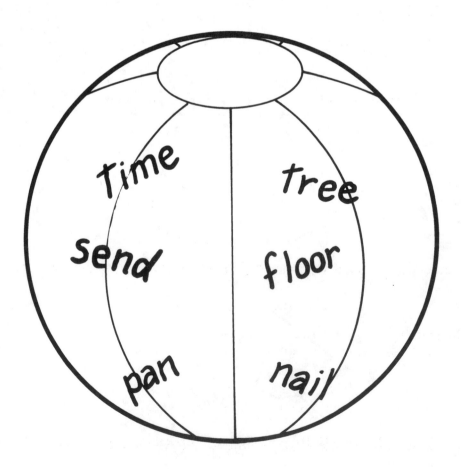

# Throwing and Catching *(cont.)*

## Materials:

- juice or vegetable cans (2 per student)
- Ping-Pong ball (1 per student)

## Can Bounce

Use two clean fruit or vegetable cans (make sure there are no sharp edges on the cans). Put a Ping-Pong ball into one can. Flip the Ping-Pong ball over your head and try to catch it in the other can. Set the timer. See who can catch it the most times in the allotted time. Challenge each student to bounce the Ping-Pong ball on a table first, then try to catch it in the can.

## Variation

Students can do a similar activity with a partner. Have students flip the Ping-Pong balls to each other. Begin by having one student toss the Ping-Pong ball with his or her hand. The other student tries to catch the Ping-Pong ball with the can. Once students can toss the Ping-Pong ball with their hands relatively easily, have each student try to flip the Ping-Pong ball out of the can for his or her partner to catch either with the hands or the can.

# Throwing and Catching *(cont.)*

## Materials:

- scoop (1 per student)
- soft foam ball (1 per student)

## Scoop It

Make a scoop by cutting away part of the bottom section of a clean, empty gallon milk jug (see diagram). Provide a soft foam ball for each student. (Be sure the ball will easily fit inside the scoop.) Begin by having two students sit opposite one another approximately 5' (150 cm) away from each other. One student rolls the ball, and the other student tries to catch the ball by scooping it up with his or her scoop. After taking the ball out of the scoop, he or she rolls the ball back toward the original student. The student can practice rolling and scooping the ball until he or she becomes skilled at catching the ball each time. Then, have students back up farther, such as 10' (3 M) away from each other.

## Materials:

- scoop (1 per student)
- beanbag or soft foam ball (1 per student)

## Scoop Catch

A student can practice throwing a ball or beanbag up in the air and catching it with the scoop. He or she holds the scoop upside-down by the handle and tries to catch the ball or beanbag into the scoop.

Pair students to play catch with each other. Begin by having students stand an arm's length (about 1' or 30 cm) apart from each other. As soon as both students successfully catch the ball in the scoop, they each take one step back. Each time both students have been successful at catching the ball or beanbag, each student takes one step backward. See how far students can get from each other.

# Throwing and Catching *(cont.)*

## Using Beanbags

Another great way to introduce students to throwing and catching is to use beanbags. Beanbags can be made any size and are not as threatening as a ball to throw or catch. Have beanbags available in a variety of textures, sizes, and colors, and allow each student to select his or her favorite one. There are a variety of ways to obtain beanbags, so don't worry if you don't sew.

### ❈ Store-Bought

Of course, beanbags can be purchased from commercial vendors. Check with your local teacher supply store, teacher supply catalogs, sporting goods stores, or sporting goods catalogs. If you order beanbags from a catalog, be sure to check the size of the beanbags so that they are appropriate for the age and size of the children you teach.

### ❈ Homemade

If you have sewing skills, making beanbags is easy to do. On pages 114–117 are simple patterns for beanbags. Be sure to keep in mind an appropriate size for your children. Simply copy the patterns onto cardboard and cut them out. Then, trace around the cardboard pattern on fabric. (This is a great way to use up scraps of fabric!) You will need two patterns for each beanbag. Use a sewing machine if possible. Face the patterns with the right sides together and sew. Be sure to leave an opening for the stuffing. Turn the beanbag right-side out and stuff with desired filling. Sew the remaining hole closed. Beans are the obvious choice for filling beanbags; however, consider some of the following fillers for a different feel: rice, packing popcorn, paper clips, pasta, sand, or wadded-up paper.

### ❈ Quick-Fix

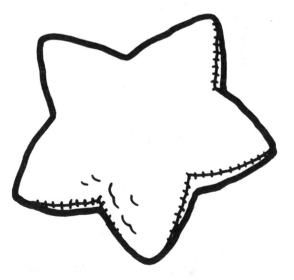

A very easy, quick way to make a beanbag is to use a plastic, resealable bag. Place beans or desired filling inside the bag. Squeeze out as much air as possible, then seal. Next, place that bag inside another plastic, resealable bag to ensure a second layer of protection from ripping. These beanbags will not hold up to the wear and tear that a young child will put on them with repeated use; however, the plastic beanbags do work well for a one-time activity or event in which you do not have easy access to sewn beanbags.

---

**Safety Note:** Be certain that an adult is always present when students are using the plastic-bag beanbags.

---

# Throwing and Catching *(cont.)*

## Bean Bag Patterns

# Throwing and Catching *(cont.)*

## Bean Bag Patterns *(cont.)*

# Throwing and Catching *(cont.)*

**Bean Bag Patterns** *(cont.)*

# Throwing and Catching (cont.)

**Bean Bag Patterns** *(cont.)*

# Throwing and Catching *(cont.)*

## Materials:

- beanbag (1 per child)

## Air Toss

Begin by having each student become familiar with how the beanbag feels. Demonstrate how to toss the beanbag up in the air just slightly (about 6" or 15 cm). Then, have the student try tossing the beanbag. Challenge him or her to toss the beanbag up in the air a little bit higher each time.

## Partner Toss

Have pairs of students face each other standing an arm's length apart. The first child tosses a beanbag to the other child. If the other child catches it, he or she tosses it back. Once both children have successfully tossed and caught the beanbag, each child takes one step backward. The pair continues tossing, catching, and stepping backward until both children miss the beanbag. If either child in the pair misses, each child takes a step toward one another.

## Hand Grab

Have each student balance his or her beanbag on the top of his or her hand. The student moves his or her hand so that the beanbag falls off, then tries to catch it with the fingers of the same hand. Have him or her begin practicing with the dominant hand, then switch to the non-dominant hand.

As the student becomes more skilled at controlling his or her throws, try the throwing and catching activities on pages 119–128.

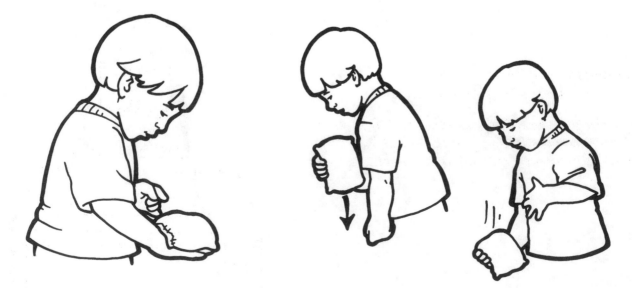

# Throwing and Catching *(cont.)*

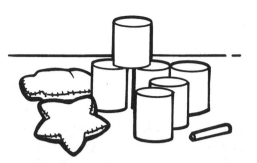

## Materials:

- 1–3 beanbags
- 6 empty cans
- chalk or masking tape

## Can Stack

Create a stack or line of soda cans on the floor. The cans may be stacked in a variety of different ways (see diagrams). Make a chalk or tape line approximately 5' (150 cm) away. Decide how many chances each student will have, and provide the appropriate number of beanbags. Have the first student stand on the line and toss the beanbag in order to knock over as many cans as possible. Have him or her count how many cans were left standing, and how many cans were knocked over before setting them back up for the next child.

If the distance is too far and students are having a difficult time knocking over the cans, move the chalk line forward. If the distance is too close, move the line backward.

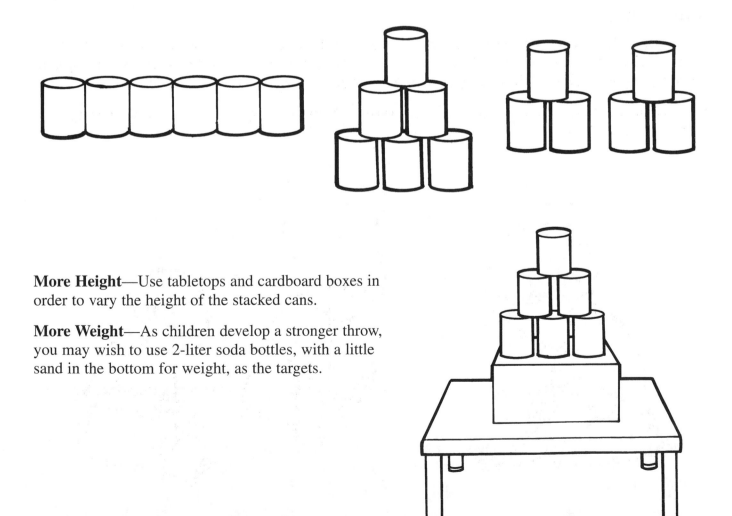

**More Height**—Use tabletops and cardboard boxes in order to vary the height of the stacked cans.

**More Weight**—As children develop a stronger throw, you may wish to use 2-liter soda bottles, with a little sand in the bottom for weight, as the targets.

# Throwing and Catching *(cont.)*

## Materials:

- Beanbag Target Patterns (See pages 121–123.)
- tagboard
- black permanent marker
- craft knife
- beanbags (3–4)

## Vertical Target Toss

### Preparation:

Choose a pattern from pages 121–123 to make into a beanbag board. Photocopy the pattern onto transparency paper. Tape a piece of tagboard on the wall. Project the transparency from an overhead projector up onto the tagboard. Trace the pattern with a black marker. Cut out appropriate holes in the pattern with a craft knife. If you wish to assign a point value for each hole, write the point value with a marker. Color the pattern if desired and laminate for durability. (If you laminate the pattern, you will have to cut the lamination out of the holes in the pattern again.)

Hang the beanbag pattern between two chairs. Have each student take a turn tossing small beanbags at the target. An adult or upper-grade student may keep score.

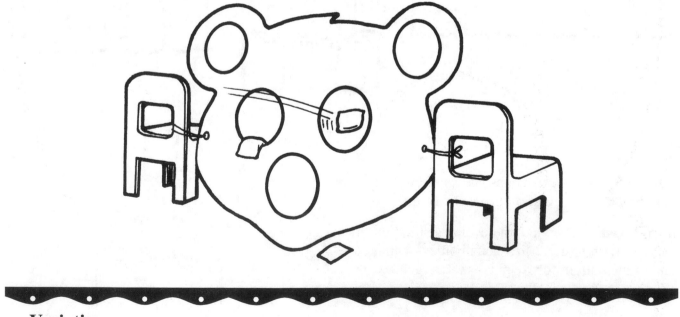

## Variation

Make the activity more challenging by having each student lie on his or her stomach while throwing the beanbag at the target, or have the student use his or her non-dominant hand to throw the beanbag.

# Throwing and Catching *(cont.)*

**Target Pattern—1**

# Throwing and Catching *(cont.)*

## Target Pattern—2

# Throwing and Catching *(cont.)*

**Target Pattern—3**

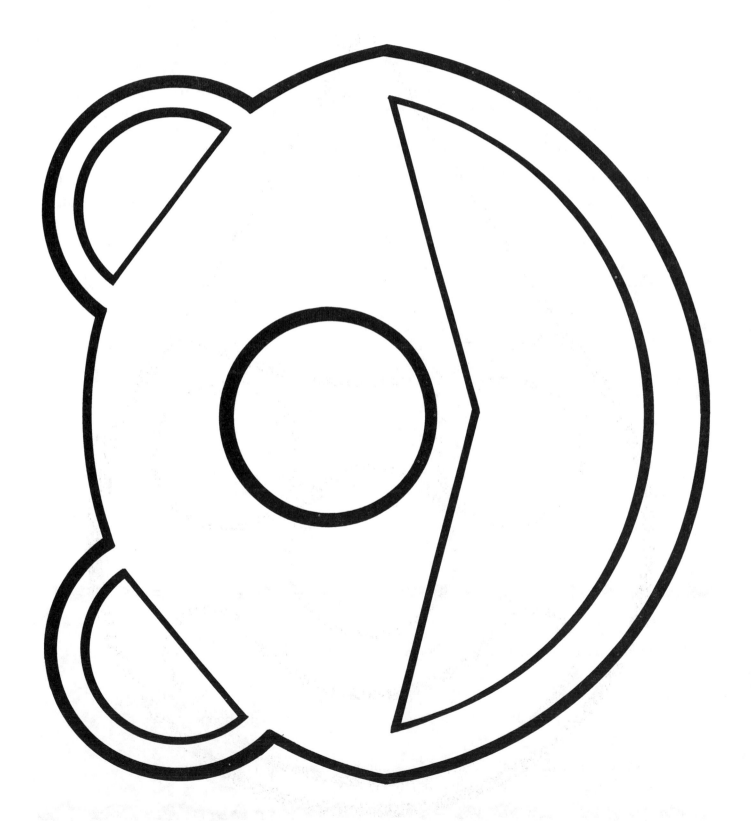

# Throwing and Catching *(cont.)*

## Materials:

- pots, pans, empty baskets, or containers
- beanbags (3–4)

## Container Toss

Make a throwing game with things you already have around the house or classroom. Gather a variety of containers. You can use pots, pans, plastic containers, boxes of different sizes, plastic bowls, etc. Gather beanbags for throwing. Set up a throwing game by placing several containers in a row at different distances. You can experiment with this part of the game, or let the children help you set it up.

Try lining up three containers in a row. A student tosses the first beanbag into the first container. Then, he or she tosses the second beanbag into the second container. Finally, the student tosses the third beanbag into the third container.

## Variations

For older students or students with a lot of control over the beanbag, use containers with small openings.

Small balls will also work for this activity. The balls create an extra challenge because students will have to really control the throw so that the balls do not bounce out of the containers.

Have students practice tossing the beanbags into hula hoops that have been laid on the ground. Arrange the hula hoops in a variety of ways.

# Throwing and Catching *(cont.)*

## Materials:

- beanbags or plastic disks
- Animal Patterns (See pages 126–127.)
- chalk

## Target Toss I

Copy the Animal Patterns on pages 126–127 onto colored cardstock. Laminate them for durability. Create a line with chalk behind which the children must stand. Place the patterns on the floor in front of the line. You may wish to tape or Velcro™ the patterns to the floor. A student tries to toss the beanbags so that they land on top of the patterns. Try a variety of arrangements for the patterns. Scatter them randomly, or try placing the patterns in a line.

# Throwing and Catching *(cont.)*

## Animal Patterns

# Throwing and Catching *(cont.)*

## Animal Patterns *(cont.)*

# Throwing and Catching *(cont.)*

## Materials:

- a beanbag or plastic disc
- chalk or tape
- paper
- pen or pencil

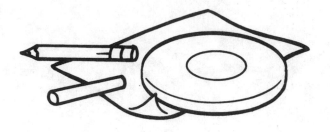

## Target Toss II

Use chalk or tape to create a circular target on the floor. Assign a point value to each part of the target. Be creative in making different patterns and point values. Have each student stand behind a tossing line and face the target. (When determining the line, take into account the students' age and abilities.) The students take turns tossing the beanbag and accruing points. Keep track of the points with a pen and paper. Play for a specific number of rounds, a predetermined point value, a certain number of tries, or just play for fun.

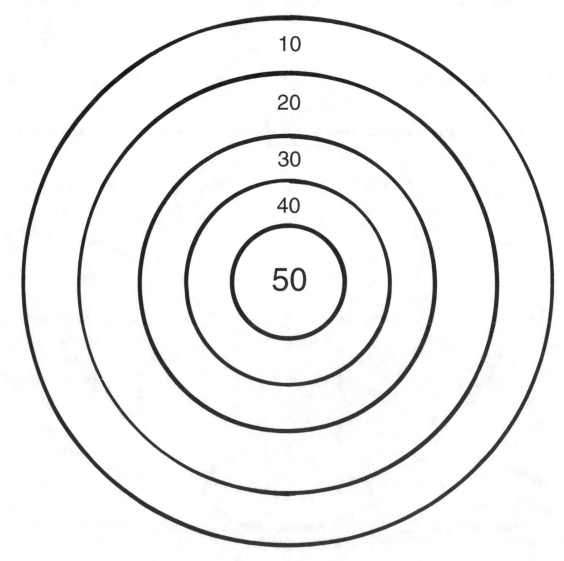

# Rolling

## Materials:

- a ball

## Ball Roll

Arrange to play this game in an area in which students can sit, in a circle (with no obstructions in the center of the circle). Have the students sit in the circle with legs crossed and knees touching. Have each student practice rolling and catching the ball across the circle.

Create a game out of the activity by having students practice a skill currently being worked on in the classroom. For example, students can practice addition while rolling the ball around the circle. A student begins the game by rolling the ball across the circle to another student. That student begins a simple math problem as he or she catches the ball by giving the first digit that will be added, such as "1." This student rolls the ball to another student who catches it and says the operation that will be used in the problem, such as "plus." The game continues with each student who catches the ball adding another piece to the equation until a student gives the solution to the problem and another problem is begun. As an example, the first problem created might be: Student #1 says "1," student #2 says "plus," student #3 says "1," student #4 says "equals," and student #5 says "2." Adapt the skill students are practicing to topics being covered in class.

For example students can practice:

- naming objects that are a particular color

- naming objects in a category (animals, food, etc.)

- the alphabet

- words that begin with the same letter

- counting forward

- counting backward

- counting by 2's, 5's, or 10's

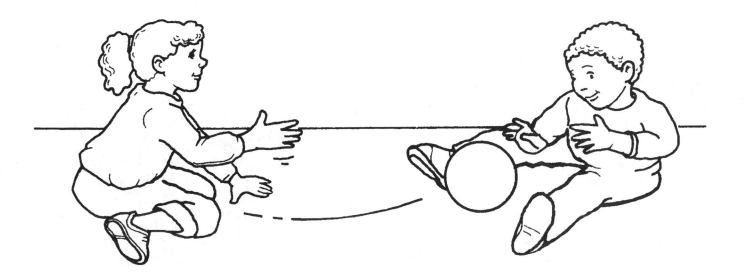

# Rolling *(cont.)*

## Materials:

- 2-liter plastic bottles (6–10 per group)

- ball (1 per group)
- sand or beans

## Bowling

Set up the 2-liter bottles as bowling pins, arranging them in a variety of ways. Begin by having the students stand about 5' (150 cm) away from the pins. A student rolls the ball in order to knock down the pins. You can have the student set up all the pins again after any are knocked down, or try to knock down any left standing before resetting them. (The second way is more difficult, so you may want to introduce this option later.) Encourage the student to try this game over and over. Make it more challenging over time by having him or her stand farther and farther back from the pins to roll the ball.

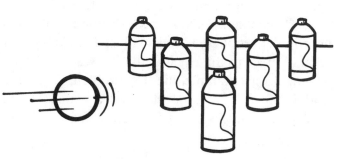

Fill the 2-liter bottles with about 1–2" (2.5–5 cm) of sand or beans. This will make the pins more difficult to knock over. A student must use more force when throwing, or a heavier ball, in order to knock down the pins.

## Materials:

- a playground ball

## Rolling in the Round

Have the students form a circle with everyone facing toward the center. Each student should stand with his or her legs spread shoulder-width apart. The student's feet should be touching the feet of the player next to him or her. Begin by tossing the ball into the circle. The object of the game is to roll the ball through another student's legs. If the ball passes through a student's legs, he or she is eliminated, and the circle becomes smaller. Play continues until there is only one student remaining.

# Kicking

## Materials:

- newspaper
- chalk or masking tape
- cardboard box

## Newspaper Kick

Use a piece of wadded-up newspaper for kicking practice. This is an excellent way to introduce kicking. It is difficult for a child to get a ball to stand still in order to kick; however, the newspaper ball will stand still. Place the ball on the floor for each student to practice kicking. Once a student is able to kick the ball, have him or her try some of these activities:

- Create a target into which the student must kick the newspaper ball. A cardboard box laid on its side is an easy and inexpensive target.

- Kick the newspaper ball back and forth between partners.

- Draw a line with chalk or place a piece of masking tape in a line on the ground. Have each student try to kick the newspaper ball along the line. Challenge him or her to keep the ball going as straight as possible. Have the student repeat the activity, this time kicking the ball next to the line. Create a curved line for the student to follow, too.

- Set up an obstacle course for each student to manipulate the newspaper ball through. Have him or her kick the ball around chairs, under desks, and through cardboard box tunnels. Have teams compete against each other in a relay, or time each student individually. See if the student can beat his or her own best time.

## Variations

As a student becomes skilled at kicking the newspaper ball, have him or her try the same activities with a real ball.

Try the same activities with a broom. A student pushes the newspaper ball along, using the broom. In this way, the student can work on arm movement.

# Batting

## Materials:

- 1 balloon

## Balloon Bounce

Arrange the children so they are standing in a circle. Bounce a balloon in the center of the circle and have the children use their hands in order to keep the balloon in the air. Challenge students to see how long they can keep the balloon in the air. Create rules with the children to establish which child will get to bounce the balloon. For example, students may not step inside the circle or, if you have a large circle, students may only take one step inside the circle. Be sure to discuss turn taking, because as the balloon comes toward two children, they will both surely go for it!

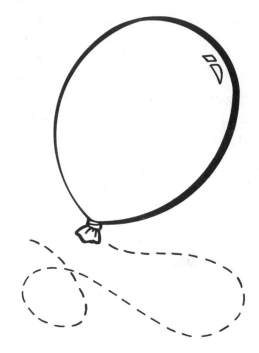

Create a game out of this activity by trying one of the suggestions below. The teacher bounces the balloon in the center of the circle and names the game requirement. For example, the teacher may say, "Counting." The first student to bounce the balloon says, "One." The next student bounces the balloon and says, "Two." If a student is unable to provide an answer, he or she has to sit down in the circle. Once all students are sitting down, begin the game again, perhaps changing the requirement. Make up your own requirements to go with your current unit of study, or use one of the variations below.

## Variations

**Alphabet**—Each student says the next letter in the alphabet.

**Colors**—The teacher names a color; each student names an object that color.

**Shapes**—The teacher names a shape; the student names an object that shape.

**Sounds**—The teacher names a letter; the student names something beginning with that letter.

**Sums**—The teacher names a sum; the student provides addends that equal the sum.

**Parts of Speech**—The teacher names a part of speech; the student provides an example.

# Batting *(cont.)*

## Materials:

- two-handed bat  (1 per child, see below for directions)
- 1 balloon

## Balloon Bop

Arrange the students in groups of four. Have one student from each group lie on his or her stomach in a circle with his or her head pointed inward.  (The students should be about 2' [61 cm] apart from each other.)  Each student holds a two-handed bat.  Toss a balloon into the center of the circle.  Using the two-handed bat, the student hits the balloon.  The object of the game is to keep the balloon in the circle.

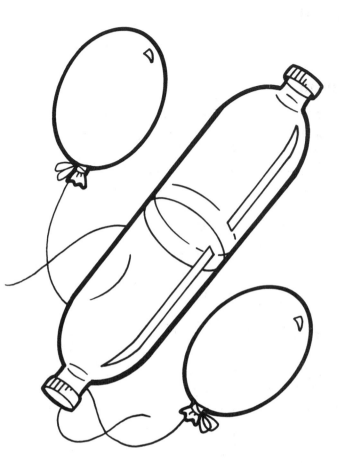

## Materials:

- two 8 oz (225 g) empty water bottles
- clear plastic wrapping tape (such as book tape)

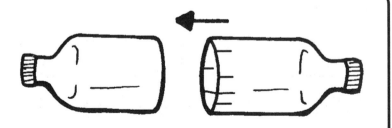

### Directions for Making a Two-Handed Bat

Cut the bottoms off two empty water bottles.  Cut six 1½" (3.84 cm) slits in the bottom of one bottle.  Push the cut ends together.  Wrap with clear wrapping tape where the ends are joined together.

# Batting *(cont.)*

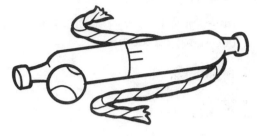

## Materials:

- 1 two-handed bat (See page 133 for directions.)
- 1 tennis ball
- 6' (182 cm) length of rope

## Tennis Ball Hit

Cut an X in a tennis ball. Tie a knot in one end of the rope, and push the knot through the X in the tennis ball. Hang the tennis ball, on the rope, from the classroom ceiling away from a wall. If your school has a tether ball pole on its playground, you may want to attach the tennis ball and rope to a tether ball pole rather than doing this activity inside.

Have each student practice hitting the tennis ball with the two-handed bat. Have the student hit the ball 10 times. If you have a group of students, students can use the rules for tether ball, but use the two-handed bats in order to hit the ball.

## Materials:

- yarn or string
- inflated balloons: green, orange, and purple

## Balloon Volleyball

Use the yarn to make a "net" by tying it to two chairs or something else that will hold it (such as a doorway, pocket chart stand, or easel). If there is a rug area for children to sit, put the yarn 3' (90 cm) from the floor. If the children are standing, place the yarn about 5' (150 cm) high.

This is an informal game where children try to bat the balloon back and forth across the net. Two balloons may be used at a time to vary the activity. A point is scored when one side fails to return the ball. The balloon can be batted as many times as necessary to return it over the net.

# Batting *(cont.)*

## Materials:

- cone
- ball
- plastic bat
- chalk

## Batting Cone

Set a ball atop a cone.  The cone will act as a stand to hold the ball.  A child uses a plastic bat to try to hit the ball off the stand.  This activity will require a lot of hand-eye coordination.  (For very young children, you may choose not to use a bat.  Simply require a child to hit the ball off the stand using his or her fist.)  Use a large ball with young children, or when introducing the activity.  As children become more skilled at successfully hitting the ball, introduce a smaller ball.

Be sure to set up this activity in a spacious area.  You may wish to create a safety zone.  Use a piece of chalk to draw a square around the batting area.  Explain to the children that they may not go into the square while another child is batting.  This will help keep all of the children safe from being hit accidentally.

Once students become skilled at successfully hitting the ball off of the cone, introduce them to Cone Ball.  (See page 136.)

**safety zone**

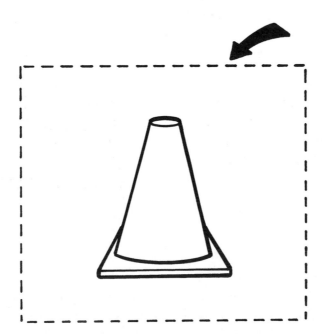

# Batting *(cont.)*

## Materials:

- cone
- ball
- bat
- 4 bases

## Cone Ball

Introduce a simple version of baseball. Set up the playing area with four bases (see diagram). The cone is set up at home plate. Divide the students into two teams, and decide which team will bat first. The other team spreads out in the outfield. When introducing this version of baseball, do not have students man the bases. In this simple version, there are no "outs." The team in the outfield is there only to catch and return the ball to home plate.

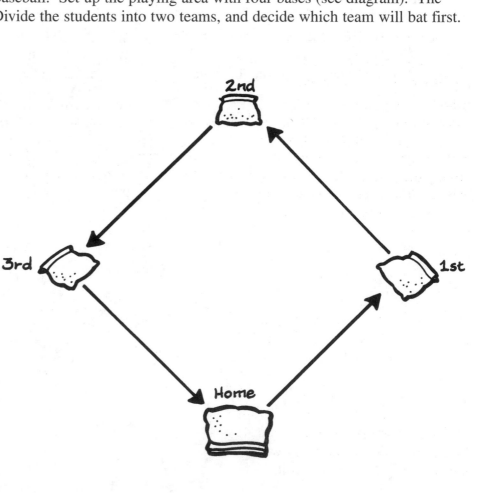

To begin playing, place the cone with a ball on it at home plate. The first player tries to hit the ball off the cone. When the ball is hit, the player runs to first base. Have him or her remain at first base until a second player has successfully hit the ball. Then, the player on first base runs to second base and the player who hits the ball runs to first base. Continue play until each child on the team has had a turn. Then, have the teams switch places.

## Hint for Making Bases

♦ Bases can be anything that outlines an area. Consider making bases out of the following: large plastic, resealable bags filled with sand, wadded-up rags, cones, carpet samples, coffee cans with sand in the bottom, or jump ropes laid out on the ground.

# Batting *(cont.)*

## Materials:

- piñata
- candy or toys
- a plastic bat or broomstick
- rope

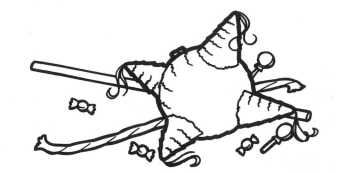

## Piñata

For holidays, celebrations, or even a normal day, a piñata can be a special treat that also provides batting practice. Purchasing a piñata is the simplest way to obtain one; however if you want to create your own, directions for an easy way to make a piñata follow on pages 138–139.

String rope through the opening at the top of the piñata. Suspend the piñata from a high point such as the ceiling, a tree branch, or a basketball goal. Be sure to explain safety procedures to the children. Establish a safety zone around the piñata. Also, make sure the children know that when the piñata is broken, they can come get the treats that fall out of it. Allow one child at a time to use a broomstick or a plastic bat to hit the piñata.

Traditionally, the player batting at the piñata is blindfolded. It will take a combination of strength and hand-eye coordination in order to break open the piñata, so if you have young children, you will probably not want to blindfold them. The idea is to provide batting practice, so the longer the piñata stays intact, the more the children will be able to practice swinging at it.

Instead of using candy, you can offer other gifts. Make or purchase inexpensive gifts (one per child). Tape a different number on each. Place the gifts in a covered box. Next, cut out squares of brightly-colored construction paper. Write a number on each so that the paper square numbers match the numbers on the gifts. Roll up each numbered square, place it in a small envelope or wrap a rubber band around the paper, and place it in the piñata as you would the candy. Once each child has a number, he or she can redeem it for a gift.

# Batting *(cont.)*

## Materials:

- a large round balloon
- strips of newspaper to cover the balloon
- whole newspaper
- flour paste
- masking tape
- string or twine
- colorful tissue paper
- peppermint or wintergreen oil (optional)
- optonal:  5 Styrofoam® cones

## Directions for Making a Piñata

These directions are for making a star-shaped piñata.  To sculpt a different-shaped piñata, change the size or shape of the balloon used, or use newspaper.

1.  Make flour paste by mixing $\frac{1}{4}$ cup (50 g) sugar and $\frac{1}{4}$ cup (50 g) flour with $1\frac{3}{4}$ cups (420 mL) water.  You may add peppermint or wintergreen oil to make the mixture smell nice.  Mix the ingredients thoroughly to avoid lumps.  Place the paste in a large bowl or tray.

2.  Blow up the balloon and tie the end closed.

3.  Dip the strips of newspaper in the paste.  Wipe off the excess while holding the strip over the bowl of paste.

4.  Wrap the strips around the balloon, leaving a small hole at the balloon opening.  Let the paper dry between the layers, and cover the balloon three or four times, letting it dry between layers.

5.  When the entire piñata is dry, prick the balloon and pull it out through the small hole.

6.  Make five cones from sheets of newspaper , or use 5 Styrofoam cones and tape them to the ball in a star pattern.  (See diagram on page 139.)

7.  Cover the entire piñata with a layer of paste and colorful tissue paper.  You may want to fringe the tissue paper and add tassels to the ends of each star point.

8.  Fill the piñata with candy or other goodies through the hole in the top, then close the hole with tape and cover with tissue paper.

9.  Cut two small parallel lines in the piñata.  Loop a piece of yarn through the opening to hang the piñata.

# Batting *(cont.)*

## Directions for Making a Piñata *(cont.)*

This is an example of how the piñata begins to take shape as you add the points of the stars.

This is a sample of the completed piñata.

# Equipment

Outside play is an extension of the classroom, and should be carefully thought out for the children's learning experiences and safety. Play, even on stationary playground equipment, can be used to teach children the full range of motions their bodies are capable of, as well as promote a healthy, active lifestyle. It is healthy for children to go outside whenever possible. Outside play should occur at least once a day, even on days that are not always ideal. Spending a little time in the rain, snow, and/or wind is good for children—just be sure they are dressed appropriately.

Through the use of equipment, both stationary (such as slides and swings) and mobile (such as jump ropes and hula hoops), students are able to gain many experiences. Children can learn many things through play, such as:

**Direction and location:** up, down, here, there, high, low, in, out, under, over, through, around

**Problem solving:** how to get from one location to the other, how to manipulate a new piece of equipment, or how to manipulate a piece of equipment in a new way

**Social skills:** turn taking, encouragement, sharing

**Body awareness:** how to manipulate their bodies in relation to the equipment, how to manipulate their bodies in relation to other children

**Imagination:** pretending

Because the equipment at each school site varies, it is difficult to provide activities which meet specific requirements. The following pages provide general safety and activity suggestions for equipment most commonly found at school sites. Take a look around your school. Oftentimes equipment purchased many years ago has been tucked in a closet. You might be surprised at what equipment you will find, not to mention new ways to use existing equipment.

# Playground Equipment

## General Safety Considerations

Playground equipment should be inspected regularly for safety. Prevention is the best medicine!

All play structures for young children should . . .

- be well-finished with smooth corners to eliminate splinters and cuts.
- be constructed with no protruding elements, such as nails or steel rods, that might cause injury.
- be placed on a shock-absorbing surface, such as sand, pea gravel, rubberized mats, or granulated pine bark. (No equipment that takes children off the ground should be on a hard surface.)
- provide children with a good balance and secure handholds as they climb up and down.
- have a safe, comfortable resting space where there is a transition to another activity (e.g., the platform at the top of a slide).
- sometimes provide alternatives to stairs and ladders. (Stairs are enjoyed by younger children, but older children like to have the opportunity to climb in other ways, such as graduated platforms or rope-netting.)

## Climbing Structures

Do not build or buy equipment for young children with a vertical fall height of greater than 8' (2.54 m) if possible. When structures bring children to levels 30" (80 cm) or more off the ground, the structures must have . . .

- protective siding corresponding to the age and size of the children. For children ages three to six years, siding should be 28–32" (70–81 cm) high.
- siding that is either solid or made of vertical boards to inhibit climbing on the siding.
- no horizontal bars that allow children to climb higher than the planned height.
- safe ways of getting from one part of the structure to another.
- a good hand grip with a rung diameter approximately $1\frac{1}{2}$" (4 cm).
- platforms with solid flooring so that sand and grit cannot fall onto children playing below.
- a design that does not place a slide and ladder parallel to each other. This prevents children from jumping from the ladder to the slide.
- no horizontal ladder or bar above or adjacent to a slide that could allow a child swinging on the ladder or bar to kick a child descending the slide.
- no open platforms adjacent to a swing.
- boards and enclosure bars that will not allow children to get their heads or arms stuck between them. (Openings of $4\frac{1}{4}$–9" [11–23 cm] can cause fatal head entrapments.)
- firm, safe connections in any rope-climbing nets or suspension nets.
- soft surfaces directly below and above 80" (2m) beyond the equipment to provide a safety zone.

---

### Safety Note

Never lift a child onto a piece of equipment that he or she cannot get off by himself or herself. When the child is ready and capable, he or she will use the equipment.

---

# Playground Equipment *(cont.)*

## Climbing Structures *(cont.)*

### Activities

When using climbing equipment, children learn how their bodies move. They develop concepts like up/down, high/low, in/out/around, over/under, and backward/sideways/forward. Children develop a sense of safety when learning to avoid moving swings, or jumping from monkey bars and landing safely in the sand. Arm and leg strength is enhanced and coordination is improved. Problem-solving skills are developed when learning to get from one place to another. From this, a sense of exploration grows. Try some of the following activities on climbing structures:

- Tie a bell on a string at the top of the climbing structure. When a student reaches the top, have him or her ring the bell.

- Have students climb to the top of the structure. Once the student can climb to the top with relative ease, have him or her count how many steps it takes to get to the top, and count how many steps it takes to get back down. Does it take more steps to climb to the top or to get back down?

- Have the student climb the structure, always leading with the same foot. For example, begin with both feet on the ground. Use the right foot to step up on the climbing structure. Then, place the left foot on the same step that the right foot was on. Then, use the right foot to take the next step. Follow the same pattern until the student has reached the top. Have him or her climb back down leading with the same foot. Then, the student tries climbing the structure with the left foot leading. If the spacing on the climbing structure allows, have the student climb the structure while alternating his or her feet.

- Challenge the student to get from one part of the climbing structure to another by taking the fewest possible steps.

- Have the student face the climbing structure while climbing it. On the way down, continue to have him or her face the same way.

# Playground Equipment *(cont.)*

## Slides

### General Safety Considerations

All slides should have. . .

- an enclosed "takeoff" platform at the top, making it virtually impossible for a child to fall.

- a barrier across the top that encourages a child to sit down to slide.

- siding 3"–6" (8–15 cm) high along the length
  of the sliding surface to prevent children from rolling off.

- no bars along the siding that can catch outstretched arms or legs.

- a slope of about 40° that will provide speed without endangering the child.

- a runoff lip at the base that promotes a smooth landing by slowing the child to a walking speed upon exit from the slide.  The lip's edge should be rounded.

- single-sheet stainless steel construction whenever possible, with longer slides carefully constructed to eliminate the chance of joints cutting children.

- a smooth sliding surface that will not wear from frequent use.

- a safety zone that extends more than 80" (2 m) beyond the runoff lip.

- a safety zone along both sides of the slide that is at least 40" (1 m) from the protective siding of the slide.

- no metal bolts or other sharp construction braces visible on the sliding surface or along the siding.

- open areas that are not exposed to direct sun for long periods of the day.  A slide should never be built with a southern exposure as surfaces will often be too hot for comfort.

---

**Safety Note**

While riding down a slide, a child should sit facing forward—never backward.

---

# Playground Equipment *(cont.)*

## Slides *(cont.)*

### Activities

Children love to go down slides. Children using slides learn turn taking, as well as vocabulary such as fast, slow, up, and down. When introducing slides to young children, be sure to select a slide that is an appropriate height and length for the age and/or size of the child. Do not force a child to climb up a slide that he or she is not willing to come down.

- The best way to begin exposing children to slides is to have them watch other children on them. Once a child is ready, have an adult go with him or her the first few times. The adult acts as a safety net when climbing to the top of the slide, as well as while coming down it. You may even want the adult to ride down the slide with the child. Cushion the child between the legs of the adult.

- Have the child climb the steps/stairs to the top of the slide. Hand him or her a stuffed animal. Have the child let the stuffed animal go down the slide. By allowing the child to control the stuffed animal, he or she will see the result of what will happen when the animal is let go.

- Have the child climb the steps or stairs to the slide and slide down into the arms of a waiting adult.

- Have the child climb up the stairs or steps of the slide, then climb back down the steps.

- Have the child climb up the slide by gripping the sides of the slide and using the arms to pull his or her body up the slide.

- Challenge the child to go down the slide as fast as he or she can, then as slowly as he or she can.

# Playground Equipment *(cont.)*

## Swings

### General Safety Considerations

All swings should have . . .

- ample space around them. Locate them in an area at least 40' by 20' (12 m x 6 m). A hedge or low fence surrounding the swings can prevent small children from running into the path of a moving swing.

- A-shaped supports framing the swing seats.

- no more than two seats attached to an individual frame to minimize bumping accidents.

- independent swinging seats hanging side by side and spaced at least 38" (1 m) apart to diminish sideways bumping.

- seats with at least 16" (41 cm) of ground clearance when in use.

- seats constructed of impact-absorbing materials or impact-absorbing surfaces on all contact areas.

- reliable fastening (shackles or fasteners, not S-hooks) on suspension mechanisms that will not open under stress, and can be secured against unauthorized loosening.

- plastic coverings over the chains.

- openings between the links of ⁵/₁₆" (8 mm) or less to prevent finger pinching.

# Playground Equipment *(cont.)*

## Swings *(cont.)*

### Activities

When swinging, children are developing their vestibular system. This system helps us to recognize where our bodies are in relation to other people or objects. Children develop hand strength and upper body strength as well. Cause and effect concepts are applied when children learn that if they let go, they will fall off the swing. Children learn to share and to take turns. Safety issues learned when going around moving swings and giving pushes to other children are encouraged. Language concepts that are utilized in swinging are high/low, fast/slow, and push. The imagination can be used to play in the swing area if others are not using the swing. Try some of the following activities:

- Have each student swing slowly, then faster.

- Once the student is swinging, challenge him or her to stop the swing as fast as possible.

- Have the student pump the swing with the legs only. Then, have the student pump the swing without using his or her legs, only the body.

- Teach students rhymes that they can sing while swinging. See the sample below. Have children make up rhymes of their own.

### Swinging High

(To the Tune of: *Goodnight Ladies*)
Swinging high,

Swinging high,

Swinging high,

I know how to swing high.

- Have the student straddle the swing in order to swing. Have him or her practice swinging side-to-side and forward and backward in this position.

- Have the student lie on his or her stomach on the swing. Have him or her draw shapes or letters in the sand below. Hide objects, such as bear counters, in the sand. Tell the student how many objects are hidden. The student must stay on the swing on his or her stomach while searching for the hidden objects.

# Playground Equipment *(cont.)*

## Tire Swings

### General Safety Considerations

No steel-belted radial tires should be used. The steel bands can eventually poke through and cause serious injury. If using such tires, make regular and thorough inspections.

Tires should have small holes every 5–6" (12–15 cm) to allow water to drain, reducing the possibility of mosquitoes or spiders in warm weather, and preventing ice in cold weather.

In Southern climates, paint tire interiors white to discourage nesting poisonous spiders.

Never place a single-point tire swing next to another kind of swing on the same support beam. In the event you use one-point pivot swings, be sure the swing cannot hit solid support beams or guard rails on structures.

### Activities

There are many different ways to use a tire swing. Children can sit in the swing in a variety of ways, such as straddling, lying, or standing. They can also move in different directions: side-to-side, back and forth, diagonally, and around. Children can swing in a steady rhythm or in a jerky manner.

Swings also encourage dialog when the teacher swings with a child, or two children ride a swing together.

- Use the activity suggestions for swings on page 146.

- Move the tire swing by shaking the rope.

- Swing in a diagonal pattern.

- Set up a beanbag target (see pages 121–123) and have the student aim a beanbag into the target while on the tire swing.

- Have the student lie on the tire swing on his or her back, then on his or her stomach.

# Playground Equipment *(cont.)*

## Tunnels

### General Safety Considerations

Only tunnels constructed in a straight line, with no bends, junctions, or vertical access connections, are acceptable.

Tunnels must have entry and exit points above the surrounding ground level, and they must be laid to facilitate drainage.

Internal diameter must be at least 40" (1 m) and the tunnel length no more than 10' (3 m).

## Activities

If you do not have a tunnel at your school site, use a cloth tunnel, or create your own tunnel following the safety recommendations above. The boxes that appliances come in are ideal for a homemade tunnel. Try some of the following activities:

- Have each student crawl through the tunnel. Direct him or her to crawl on his or her knees using the hands to move along. Then, have the student crawl through the tunnel without using his or her hands.

- If the tunnel is stable, have the student crawl on top of, or over, the tunnel.

- Have the student walk through the tunnel. He or she will have to crouch down in order to do this.

- Set up a target (see pages 121–123) about 3' (90 cm) in front of one end of the tunnel. The student picks up a beanbag, then crawls through the tunnel. Before coming out the other side, the student has to throw the beanbag at the target.

# Playground Equipment *(cont.)*

## Rocking Equipment

### General Safety Considerations

All rocking equipment should . . .

- allow the young child to initiate and control the rocking motion.

- ensure that limbs cannot be pinched, or trapped, in the spring of the equipment.

- provide the child with comfortable and secure handholds and seating positions.

- provide side-to-side as well as back-and-forth rocking motions for increased challenge.

### Activities

- Have the child rock slowly, then faster.

- Once the child is rocking, have him or her stop the piece of equipment as quickly as possible.

- Have the child rock only in a forward motion, or only in a backward motion. Because of the spring in the rocking equipment, there will be both forward and backward motion; however, the idea is to have the child control the rocking equipment to produce a particular type of movement.

- Have the child hold a beanbag in each hand while rocking on the piece of equipment. Have him or her rock forward and backward 10 times each while counting out loud. When the student reaches 10, he or she throws the beanbags up into the air. The child can do this one at a time, or together if he or she can balance well on the rocking equipment.

- Set up a target (see pages 121–123) for the child to throw beanbags at while rocking on the piece of equipment.

# Playground Equipment *(cont.)*

## Riding Toys

### General Safety Considerations

All riding equipment should have . . .

- adequate air in the tires.

- seats and pedals appropriate for the age of the children.

- comfortable and secure handholds and seating positions.

- a good surface on which to ride, such as cement or a packed dirt track.

- appropriate safety devices, such as helmets and training wheels (depending on the age and ability of the children).

- chains that are well-lubricated and fit securely on the riding equipment.

- no metal bolts or other sharp construction visible.

- a shady area to park equipment. Metal riding equipment, in particular, needs to be kept out of the sun when not in use, as surfaces will often be too hot for comfort.

# Playground Equipment *(cont.)*

## Riding Toys *(cont.)*

### Activities

When children play on riding toys, they learn strength, balance, and large muscle coordination. Children use their energy in a constructive manner. They develop concepts of speed, direction, and location. Children use their imaginations as they pretend to be different characters and make different "road" noises. Language development is enhanced with this kind of play. Riding toys allow children to learn to negotiate, take turns, and solve problems. They gain self-confidence in learning and mastering new skills.

- Have the student ride fast, then slow, then fast again.

- Play a version of Red Light, Green Light. At a whistle signal or the verbal command, "Green Light," students ride on the equipment. When the whistle is blown again, or the leader says, "Red Light," students must come to a complete stop on their riding equipment. Continue the game so that students gain plenty of practice in starting and stopping the riding equipment.

- Create an obstacle course for each student to ride the equipment around, through, over, and under.

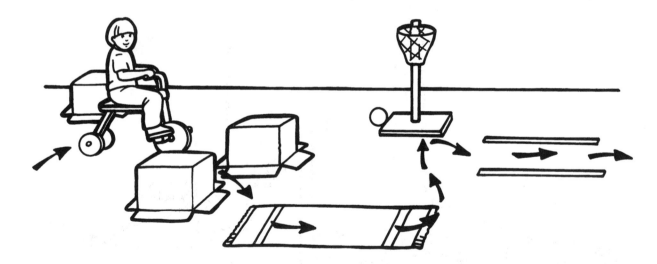

- Have the student determine a noise and a honking sound that his or her riding equipment will make. The student rides around the track making the selected noise. Each time the student comes to another student, he or she must give that honking sound.

- Have the student ride around the track. Each time he or she gets back to a predetermined starting point, have the student get off the equipment and perform a task. The task can be as simple as doing 10 jumping jacks, as complex as painting a picture, or as fun as eating a snack.

- Set up a target (see pages 121–123). Have each student ride around the track with a beanbag in his or her hand. When the student gets to the target, he or she can stay on the piece of riding equipment, or get off and stand in order to throw the beanbag at the target.

- Provide sponges and water for the student to wash the riding equipment.

# Parachutes

## Materials:

- parachute

Parachute play is a great way to get everyone to play together. Usually, you will have full participation when you bring out a parachute. Parachutes intrigue even the most reluctant of children, encouraging them to participate. Parachutes can be purchased commercially, but if you don't have your own you can use a sheet (cut in a circle), or an old, round table cloth for most of the activities.

To begin, arrange the students in a circle around the perimeter of the parachute. If the parachute has handles, students can hold onto them. If the parachute does not have handles, students can simply roll up the edge of the parachute in order to hold it in their hands. Then, try a variety of activities. Some suggestions are listed on this page and pages 153–155.

## Circles

Students simply walk in a circle (holding the parachute), first clockwise, then counterclockwise. Each student can use both hands at first, then, just the left hand, then just the right hand. Have the students try running, skipping, or hopping in a circle. Have them practice counting by 1's, 2's, 5's, or 10's while walking in the circle. In addition, students can recite rhymes or the alphabet.

## Circle Activities

Have each student walk in a circle while holding the parachute with one hand. Provide another activity for the student to do with the other hand, such as lifting the hand over head or bouncing a ball. Be sure to alternate the direction in which the student walks, thus altering the hand that each student must use to dribble the ball.

## Waves

Have each student shake the parachute in order to make waves. Describe the kind of waves you want him or her to make. For example, each student can make gentle waves or rough waves. Begin by having the student use both hands to make the waves. Then, have him or her use only the right hand. Then, have the student use only the left hand.

# Parachutes (cont.)

## Materials:

- parachute
- radio, cassette, or CD player

## High/Low

Students raise the parachute as high in the air as possible. Then, students lower the parachute all the way to the ground. Have students try this same activity while in a variety of body positions. For example, students can lie on their stomachs facing the parachute while raising the parachute as high as possible and then back to ground level, or students can kneel on the ground while completing a task.

## Tents

Once students know how to do High/Low, show them how to make a tent. Students raise the parachute as high as possible. While raising the parachute in the air, each student takes one step toward the middle of the circle. Then, students lower the parachute, pulling it behind their backs as they sit down. At this point, they will be underneath the parachute. (The parachute will make a domed tent over their heads.) Once the dome has collapsed, have the students repeat the action.

## Music March

Play a song. Have each student determine how the music makes him or her feel and what movements he or she could do with the parachute that matches the music. Begin by using songs that the students are familiar with. Then, try songs they may not have heard. Be sure to try a variety of different types of music including: jazz, classical, and rock and roll.

## The Scoot

Have students sit on the ground around the parachute. Each student should put his or her legs straight out in front so that the legs are underneath the parachute. The students hold the parachute until it is taut. While holding onto the parachute, students should scoot toward the center of the circle. (Beforehand, determine how many scoots the children should do. The parachute will become loose as the children scoot toward the middle of the circle.) Then, have the students scoot backward until the parachute is taut again. They can also kick their feet at different speeds under the parachute.

# Parachutes *(cont.)*

## Materials:

- parachute
- stuffed bunny (or other stuffed animal)

## Jumping Bunnies

Place a stuffed bunny (or other stuffed animal) in the center of the parachute. Have each student take hold of the parachute. Students make the bunny jump up in the air by bringing their arms up at the same time, then quickly bringing their arms down. Have students count how many times they can bounce the bunny in the air without letting it jump out of the parachute.

## Materials:

- parachute
- 3–4 balls

## Ball Bounce

Begin by placing only one ball in the middle of the parachute. After each student has taken hold of the parachute, have him or her bounce the parachute up and down in order to bounce the ball. The object is to keep the ball in the parachute. Once students have the idea, place several balls in the parachute. If one falls out, have a student retrieve the ball and throw it back into the parachute.

Divide the students into two teams, one team on each half of the parachute. Place one ball in the center of the parachute. A team scores a point by bouncing the ball off the other team's side of the parachute. Play to a predetermined number of points.

# Parachutes *(cont.)*

## Materials:

- 2 parachutes
- 24 Styrofoam balls (2" diameter or 5 cm)

## Popcorn Game I

Purchase colored Styrofoam balls or spray paint white Styrofoam balls. Divide the children into two groups. Place each group evenly around a parachute. Have each child grip the parachute around the edges. For warm-up, have the children shake the parachute vigorously. To play the game, place 12 Styrofoam balls on each parachute. The first team to shake all the balls off its parachute wins the game.

## Materials:

- a parachute
- 16 Styrofoam balls (2" diameter or 5 cm)

## Popcorn Game II

Purchase colored Styrofoam balls or spray paint white Styrofoam balls (e.g., eight each of red and blue). Divide the children into two teams. Place them evenly around the parachute with one team standing around one half of the parachute, and the other half standing around the other half of the parachute. Assign each team a color of Styrofoam ball. Each child shakes the parachute, trying to keep his or her team's color of ball on the parachute while trying to bounce off the other team's balls. The first team to shake off all of the opponents' balls is the winner.

# Hula Hoops

## Materials:

- hula hoop (1 per child)

## Hula Hoop Activities

Hula hoops are another piece of equipment which instantly gain students' attention and interest. Allow plenty of time for free exploration when introducing hula hoops to students. Have a student demonstrate how to rotate the hula hoop around his or her waist. Students can practice trying to hula hoop in the traditional manner; however, there are plenty of activities students can do with the hula hoop, even if they have not mastered rotating it around their waists.

- Have each student raise his or her arms to the side and use them to rotate the hula hoop around his or her wrists, rotating the hula hoop forward, then backward. Have the student try doing this activity with the dominant arm, as well as the non-dominant arm. Challenge him or her to raise the arm overhead and rotate the hula hoop horizontally overhead.

- Pretend the hula hoop is a large steering wheel. Have each student hold the hula hoop so his or her hands are positioned at 2 o'clock and 10 o'clock. Have him or her loosen the grip so that the hula hoop can slip through the hands while rotating it (hands should remain at the 2 o'clock and 10 o'clock position). Then, tell the student to rotate the hula hoop through his or her hands in order to turn the hula hoop in a circle. Have him or her turn the hula hoop clockwise, then counterclockwise and try to rotate the hula hoop so that the hands have to move. Direct the student to rotate the hoop by moving hand over hand to move it clockwise; he or she can reverse the hoop to move it in a counterclockwise direction. (Put a tape mark at 12 o'clock so he or she can see the movements.)

- Have the student rotate the hula hoop around the neck.

- Put the hula hoop on the ground. The student places the right foot in the hula hoop, resting the front part of the hoop on the top of the shoe. He or she rotates the hula hoop around the leg. Each time the hula hoop comes to the left foot, the student jumps over the hoop. Once a momentum has been built up, it is easy to continue.

# Hula Hoops *(cont.)*

## Materials:

- hula hoop (1 per child)

## Activities

- Do the Hokey Pokey (see page 23) with the hula hoop. A student performs the actions of the song by putting the body part mentioned in each verse in the hula hoop. For example:

    "You put your right arm in." (Student holds the hula hoop in a manner which allows him or her to place his or her right arm in the center of the hula hoop.)

    "You put your right arm out." (Student removes his or her arm from the hula hoop.)

    "You put your right arm in and you shake it all about." (Student puts his or her right arm back in the center of the hoop, then shakes the arm.)

- Create groups of four students. Each group of students stands around the outside of a hula hoop while holding onto it with the hands. Have the group walk around in a circle both clockwise and counterclockwise. Students will have to work together in order to perform this activity.

- Place the hula hoop on the ground. Have each student move around the outside of the hula hoop in the following ways:

| | | | |
|---|---|---|---|
| clockwise | hopping | on tiptoes | marching |
| counterclockwise | jumping | on heels | walking |

- Place the hula hoop on the ground. A student jumps in and out of the hula hoop upon hearing a signal. For example, the student begins inside the hoop. When he or she hears a whistle blow, the student jumps out of the hula hoop. When the student hears the whistle again, he or she jumps back inside the hula hoop.

- Place the hula hoop on the ground. Help each student become aware of his or her own body space by having him or her jump in and out of the hula hoop with a partner. Begin by having both partners step in and out of the hula hoop. Then, after a little practice, the partners can jump in and out of the hoop. Each student will really have to be aware of how much space he or she is taking up, and how much space is left for his or her partner when both are in the hoop.

# Hula Hoops *(cont.)*

## Materials:

- 4–6 hula hoops
- chalk or a jump rope

## Hula Jump

Arrange 4–6 hula hoops on the ground in a straight line. Create a starting line with a jump rope or a piece of chalk. Have each student jump from one hula hoop to the other. The student must land with both feet inside the hula hoop and jump in each of the hula hoops. When he or she gets to the end, the student turns around and jumps back to the starting line.

## Variations

Try arranging the hula hoops in a variety of different positions.

Have each student leap or hop, instead of jump.

Spread out several hula hoops in a large space in your classroom. Give each student several beanbags. Have him or her toss one beanbag into each of the hoops.

# Hula Hoops *(cont.)*

## Materials:

- hula hoop (1 per child or group)

## Hula Hoop Roll

Place the hula hoop in a vertical position. (The bottom of the hula hoop should be touching the ground.) Each child's hands should be positioned so that they are gripping the top of the hula hoop. Have the child roll the hula hoop along the ground by pushing the hoop along with his or her hands. He or she will need to use the hands to steady the hula hoop. Try some of these activities:

Have partners roll the hula hoop back and forth to each other.

Create an obstacle course for children to roll the hula hoop through.

Have a relay to see who can roll his or her hula hoop to a particular destination the fastest.

Use a stick, ruler, or unsharpened pencil to push the hula hoop along.

## Materials:

- hula hoop (1 per child)
- chalk or a beanbag

## Challenge Roll

Place the hula hoop in a vertical position. (The bottom of the hula hoop should be touching the ground.) The child's hands should be positioned so that he or she is gripping the top of the hula hoop. If the child flicks his or her wrists forward quickly, then releases the hula hoop, the hula hoop will roll forward.

Once the child gets the idea of how to flick his or her wrists in order to make the hula hoop roll forward, challenge him or her to see how far the hula hoop can roll. Create a starting line with a piece of chalk. Have the child roll the hula hoop as far as possible. He or she can use chalk or a beanbag to mark where the hula hoop fell over.

# Hula Hoops *(cont.)*

## Materials:

- hula hoop (1 per group)
- radio, cassette, or CD player

## Hoop Teams

Divide the students into teams of four and assign each group a hula hoop. (Assigning each group a particular color of hula hoop works well if you have a variety of colors available.) Randomly place as many hula hoops as there are groups around the room or playing area. Explain to each student that he or she is to move around the room safely while the music plays. When the music stops, the student moves to his or her team's hula hoop. Teams must work cooperatively so that each member of the team has a body part inside its hoop.

## Variations

Announce the part of the body that students must have in the hula hoop.

Do the activity with the directions that each team member must have two body parts inside the hula hoop.

# Jump Ropes

## Materials:

- jump rope (1 per group)

## Crossing the River

Create groups of 4–6 children. Select two children to be jump rope holders. Each of these children holds the end of a jump rope and pulls it taut so there is not any slack in the rope. The jump rope will be the "river." The jump rope holders begin with the rope very low to the ground. (Two students can lay the jump rope on the ground, but still hold the ends taut.) The remaining children will be runners. They run from where they are standing over to the other side of the river. When the children get to the river, they must jump or hop over it. Then, the two jump rope holders raise the rope about 2" (8 cm). The runners then try to cross the river again by jumping over the rope. The jump rope holders continue raising the rope until students are unable to jump or hop across the river.

## Variations

### Rippling River

The students holding the jump rope wave the rope gently back and forth. Students try to jump or hop over the river without touching the rope.

### Wavy Water

The students holding the jump rope wave the rope with more force. Students try to jump or hop over the river without touching the rope.

# Jump Ropes *(cont.)*

## Materials:

- jump rope (1 per group)

## Helicopter

One student from each group is selected to be the "helicopter." The helicopter stands in the middle of a circle formed by the remaining students (the "jumpers"). The jumpers need to stand back far enough so that they take one step forward in order to jump the rope at the appropriate time. If the jumpers stand too close, they will get hit with the flying jump rope. The helicopter begins by holding one end of the jump rope in his hand, and swinging it in a circle over his or her head. All of the students recite the following poem:

### Helicopter, Helicopter

Helicopter, helicopter turn around,

Helicopter, helicopter touch the ground.

*(The helicopter touches the ground.)*

Helicopter, helicopter do a trick,

Helicopter, helicopter count like this . . . 1, 2, 3, 4, 5 . . .

When the poem has been recited and the counting begins, the helicopter lowers the jump rope so that it drags on the floor in a circle. The students standing around the circle take one step toward the middle of the circle. As the jump rope comes toward them, they have to jump over it. As each child jumps over the rope, he or she counts off a number. See how many jumps can be made before a student misses.

# Jump Ropes *(cont.)*

## Materials:

- a shot rope (1 per group)

## Jump the Shot Rope

Jumping the shot rope is an excellent introduction to jumping rope. Students can practice jumping over the rope without having to worry about turning the rope.

Arrange the children in groups of five. Each group of children makes a circle. Place one student in the middle of the circle and have him or her hold onto this rope at the end opposite the tennis ball. The student in the middle squats down and spins the rope, while the rest of the children in the circle jump over the shot (rope with a ball attached to it) as it passes. The student in the middle can turn five to six times, then switch positions. See page 162 for a "helicopter" game that can be played with a shot rope.

## Materials:

- tennis ball
- craft knife
- 7' (212 cm) rope

## Directions for Making a Shot Rope

Using a craft knife, cut an X into a tennis ball. The slits forming the X should be approximately 1" (2.54 cm) long. Tie a knot in one end of the rope and push the knot through the X in the tennis ball.

# Jump Ropes *(cont.)*

## Materials:

- Jump Rope Rhymes (See below and pages 165–166.)
- jump rope (1 per student)

## Jump Rope Rhymes

Teach students the jump rope rhymes. Then, have students sing the rhymes while they practice jumping rope. You can do this activity with each child using his or her own rope. Or, you can use a long jump rope. Place one child at each end of the jump rope to turn it while a third child in the middle jumps the rope.

## Counting Song

Number one, touch your tongue.

Number two, touch your shoe.

Number three, touch your knee.

Number four, touch the floor.

Number five, learn to jive.

Number six, pick up sticks.

Number seven, go to heaven.

Number eight, shut the gate.

Number nine, touch your spine.

Number ten, do it all again!

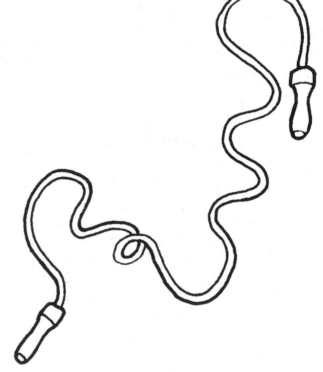

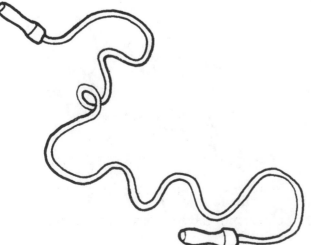

## Jumping Rope

*(To the Tune of: "Goodnight Ladies")*

Jumping rope,

Jumping rope,

Jumping rope,

Won't you do it, too?

# Jump Ropes *(cont.)*

## Jump Rope Rhymes *(cont.)*

### Sailor Rhyme

Have you ever, ever, ever

In your long-legged life

Seen a long-legged sailor

Kiss his long-legged wife?

No, I never, never, never,

In my long-legged life

Saw a long-legged sailor

Kiss his long-legged wife.

### Teddy Bear

Teddy bear, teddy bear, turn around,

Teddy bear, teddy bear, touch the ground.

Teddy bear, teddy bear, turn out the light,

Teddy bear, teddy bear, say, "Good-night."

### Can You Do This?

*(To the Tune of: "Are You Sleeping?")*

Can you do this? Can you do this?

Look at me. Look at me.

Everybody try it, everybody try it.

You will see. You will see.

### Come Jump Rope

*(To the Tune of: "Skip to My Lou")*

Come, come, come jump rope,

Come, come, come jump rope,

Come, come, come jump rope,

It is lots of fun.

# Jump Ropes *(cont.)*

## Jump Rope Rhymes *(cont.)*

### Having Fun

*(To the Tune of: "The More We Get Together")*

We are jumping rope, jumping rope, jumping rope.

We are jumping rope.

We're having so much fun.

There's (child's name) and (child's name)
and (child's name) and (child's name).

We are jumping rope.

We're having so much fun.

### Hippity Hop

Hippity-hop to the barbershop

To buy a stick of candy.

One for you and one for me,

And one for sister Mandy.

### Playmates

Oh, little playmate,

Come out and play with me.

And bring your dollies three.

Climb up my apple tree.

Slide down my rainbow,

Into my cellar door.

And we'll be jolly friends,

Forevermore, more, more.

So sorry, playmate,

I cannot play with you.

My dolly has the flu,

Boo-hoo, boo-hoo, boo-hoo.

I've got no rainbow.

I've got no cellar door.

But we'll be jolly friends

Forevermore, more, more.

# Combining Equipment

## Materials:

- Movement Activity Cards
  (See page 168 for directions.)

- Paused Music
  (See page 168 for directions.)

- cassette/radio player

- equipment (determined by which
  movement cards you will be using)

## Movement Centers

Determine which Movement Activity Cards you will be using. Gather the equipment appropriate for those cards. Divide students into as many groups as there are cards. Spread the cards out around the area you will be using so that students have plenty of room to move. Have each group of children stand next to a different card. Play a Paused Music tape. The group moves, following the directions on its card. When the tape comes to a pause (a point at which there is no music), the group rotates clockwise to a new center. When the music begins again, the group begins doing the movement at its new center. Continue until the music ends, or until each group has been to each center.

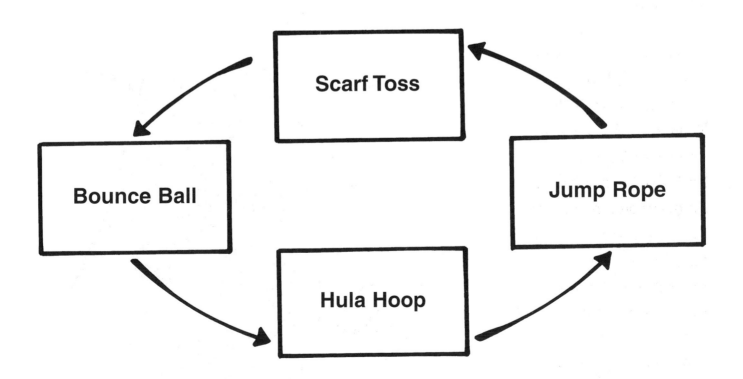

# Combining Equipment *(cont.)*

## Materials:

- transparency film
- tagboard
- overhead projector
- markers
- crayons or colored pencils

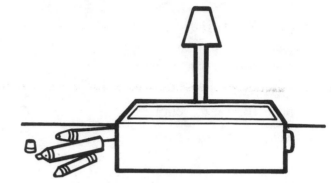

## Making Movement Activity Cards

Make Movement Activity Cards (see pages 169–171) by enlarging or photocopying the pages onto transparency film. Project the transparency onto a piece of tagboard. Trace the images onto the tagboard with a marker. Color and laminate if desired. The Movement Activity Cards on the following pages include equipment used in activities provided in other areas of this book. For example, a jump rope card is provided; however, activities for a jump rope are listed in the "Locomotor Skills" section of this book under Jumping. Create your own movement cards based on the equipment you have available, and the activities that you would like your students to complete.

## Materials:

- 2 cassette/radio players or 1 double-deck cassette/radio player
- 1 audio tape
- music (tape or radio)

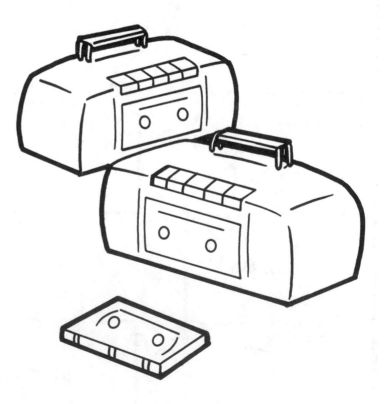

## Making Paused Music

Make a recording of music that has pauses about every minute or two (approximately 20 minutes total playing time). In order to do this, play music on one tape. Record the songs on another tape. Once you hit record, do not stop recording until you have reached the end of a song. About every minute or two, pause the music for 10–15 seconds. Then, play the music again for one minute. Pause again for 10–15 seconds. Continue until the end of the music you wish to tape. The result will be a recording of music with breaks (for transitions).

# Combining Equipment (cont.)

**Movement Activity Cards**

# Combining Equipment *(cont.)*

**Movement Activity Cards**

# Combining Equipment (cont.)

**Movement Activity Cards**

# Sensory Tables

Sensory tables provide children with an opportunity to experiment and play with a variety of textures. Children learn naturally through their senses, so it makes sense to use these activities daily in the classroom. There are a variety of ways to provide sensory table experiences for young children. Consider some of the options mentioned in this section as you plan experiences for your students.

Of course, you can commercially purchase sensory tables for classroom use. These tables are specifically designed for the types of activities described on the next few pages. If, however, the cost of purchasing a sensory table is prohibitive, don't worry, there are alternatives to providing sensory table activities at a more affordable price.

Ideas for sensory table alternatives:

- table tops
- cookie sheets
- large plastic bowls
- plastic tubs
- aluminum roasting pans
- gift boxes

The advantage of the alternatives to sensory tables mentioned above is that they are small enough for use inside a classroom. Many of the commercially bought sensory tables are designed for outdoor use. If you do set up a sensory table inside the classroom, it is a good idea to place a towel or piece of plastic underneath the table. The towel or plastic will act as a drop cloth to make clean up much easier.

When selecting a surface on which students will be doing sensory table activities, consider the type of activity that the children will be doing, and the type of material in the sensory table. For example, a cookie sheet will not make a good water sensory table; however, it would work well with salt in it.

Ideas for sensory table contents:

- sand
- water
- beans (all varieties)
- rice
- shaving cream
- noodles
- packing popcorn
- cornmeal
- shredded paper

**Safety Note:** Be sure to monitor the contents of the sensory table. The contents will have to be dumped and replaced depending on how often and how many children use the sensory table.

# Sand

Most students will already be familiar with playing in a sandbox. You will want to set some guidelines when using sand in a sensory table for the first time. Be sure students know that they should try to keep the sand in the sensory table. Of course, sand will inevitably end up out of the sensory table; however be sure students know the goal is to keep the sand inside. When the sand does end up on the floor outside the sensory table, provide a small broom and dustpan and have the children help clean up the over-spill. The act of sweeping up the sand in and of itself is great motor skill practice. Also, be sure that students know that sand in the eyes will hurt.

Following are some guidelines for a safe sandbox or sensory table. The sand should be:

- 15–18" (38–46 cm) deep.

- "packable" when moist and able to hold shapes well.

- a balanced mixture of particles, ranging from very fine to coarse, with coarse particles no larger than $1/16$" (1.5 mm).

- free of any sharp materials, such as artificially crushed stone.

- washed so it is clean and free of clay, silt, oxides, iron, or other contaminates. (Before accepting sand delivery, test it by placing a sample on a white cloth to see if the sand stains or discolors it. Discoloration or stain indicates the sand has not been washed sufficiently.)

# Sand *(cont.)*

## Materials:

- sandbox or sensory table filled with sand
- sand toys (see below)

## Sand Toys

You will want to make some general-use sand toys available at all times, including buckets and shovels. However, spark student interest in using the sandbox or a sensory table filled with sand by changing the types of toys available for students. It is easiest to remember to change toys if you have a rotation schedule set up and a list of ideas for toys. For example, you may want to make a schedule to collect sand toys each Friday and get some new surprises ready. Keep this list handy for some fun ideas!

- balance scale
- beans (to mix with sand)
- berry baskets
- birthday candles
- blocks
- bowls
- buckets
- cars
- colanders
- cookie cutters
- craft sticks
- cups
- dinosaurs
- egg cartons
- envelopes
- feathers
- film canisters
- flower pots
- funnels
- gloves (to wear)
- ice cube trays
- measuring cups and spoons
- mittens (to wear)

- muffin tins
- nesting toys
- nuts
- paper bags
- pasta shapes
- pie plates
- plastic eggs
- rubber gloves (to fill with sand)
- salt and pepper shakers
- sand wheels
- scoops
- shells
- shovels
- small trucks
- spray bottles (to make sand wet)
- strainers
- Styrofoam packing pieces
- tongs
- toy trees
- tweezers (large)
- wooden animals

# Sand *(cont.)*

## Materials:

- sandbox or sensory table filled with sand
- funnel
- large plastic cups (2 per child)
- cups and pitchers of different sizes

## Funnel Pour

Have a child place a funnel securely in the top of a cup. Next, have him or her scoop up some dry sand in another cup and slowly pour it into the funnel. After the cup of sand has been poured through the funnel, have him or her remove the funnel and place it on the now empty cup. Using the cup of sand, the child pours the sand through the funnel into the other cup. Encourage each child to repeat this activity, pouring the sand back and forth through the funnel from cup to cup several times.

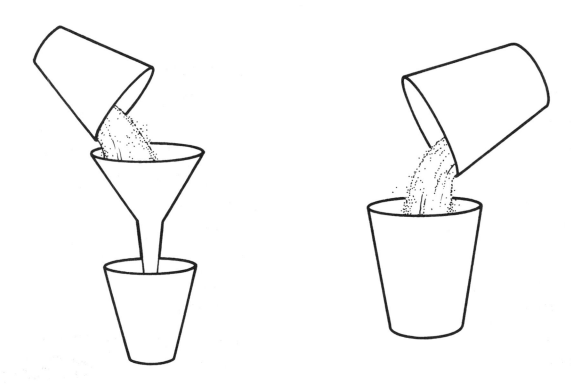

This activity can be done without a funnel. Use a variety of different-sized and shaped containers or cups. Have each child practice pouring sand from one container to the other, then back into the sandbox or sensory table.

By using cups or pitchers of different sizes and shapes, the children will begin to grasp the concept that the same amount of a substance looks like a different amount in a different-sized container.

# Water

## Materials:

- small pool, tub, or sensory table filled with water
- toys
- towels
- mat or indoor/outdoor carpet

## Water Fun

Experimenting with water is one activity you will not have any trouble getting kids involved in, especially if it does not involve taking a bath! Provide a sensory table filled with water for students to use for experimenting. If you do not have access to a sensory table for water fun, try using a small pool or plastic tub. Be prepared for students to get a little wet whenever water is involved, and have bath towels available for overspills.

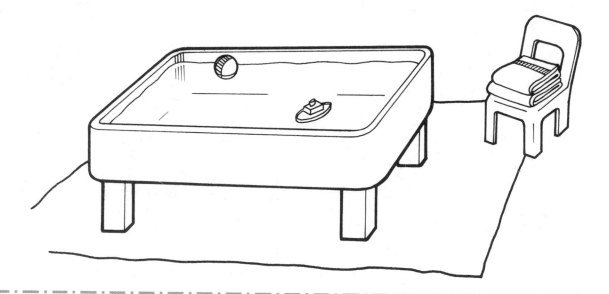

## Safety Notes

- ◆ An adult must be posted at any activity involving water. It is possible for a child to drown in even 1" (2.5 cm) of water, so the greatest caution should be taken for a safe, pleasurable experience.

- ◆ Water in a water table must be changed daily.

- ◆ Tables should always be emptied when not in use.

- ◆ Have a mat with rubber backing or some indoor/outdoor carpeting under the water table/tub, where the children will be standing, to prevent the floor from getting slippery.

# Water *(cont.)*

## Materials:

- small pool, tub, or sensory table filled with water
- water toys (see below)

## Water Toy Fun

Encourage experimentation and creativity by varying the types of toys available to children when they come to the water station. Listed below are ideas for items which can be used in a water station. Most of the items can be found around your home or classroom.

| | | |
|---|---|---|
| aquarium rocks | plastic eggs | straws |
| aquarium plants | plastic fish and fishing pole | Styrofoam trays |
| berry baskets | plastic toys | tongs |
| bowls | rubber gloves with pin holes (for water to leak) | toothbrushes |
| dosage spoons | salt and pepper shakers | tweezers |
| eggbeater | scoops | washcloths |
| eye droppers | shells | water wheels |
| fish nets | slotted spoons | watering cans |
| funnels | soup spoons | whisks |
| measuring cups/spoons | sponges | wind-up toys |
| nesting toys | squeeze bottles | wooden ladles |
| pitchers | squirt bottles | |
| plastic bottle with pin holes | strainers | |

Try adding some of the suggestions below to the water to change the texture, appearance, or smell.

- baking soda
- beans
- birdseed
- bubble solution
- liquid detergent
- cornmeal
- cornstarch
- crushed ice

- dry leaves
- extracts (for smell)
- flour
- food coloring
- glitter
- dry oats
- O-shaped cereal
- pasta
- plain and colored ice cubes

- popped popcorn
- potting soil
- pumpkin pulp and seeds
- rice
- salt
- sequins
- shaving cream
- wood shavings

# Water *(cont.)*

## Materials:

- small pool, tub, or sensory table filled with water
- eggbeater
- mild liquid soap

## Eggbeater Bubbles

It is ideal to do this activity in a small pool, plastic tub, or sensory table filled with water; however, it can also be done with a large bowl set on a non-skid placemat. Fill the container ¹/₃ full of cold water. Add a few tablespoons of liquid soap and place the eggbeater in the bowl, resting it on the bottom. Demonstrate for the children how to use an eggbeater (since many will probably not have seen one before). Then, let each child take a turn making bubbles.

## Materials:

- washcloth (1 per child)
- bar of soap

## Magic Bubble Cloth

Distribute washcloths to the students and explain that each student should use his or her own washcloth. Have the student wet the washcloth, then squeeze it out a little bit. Rub some soap lightly on a small area, in the center, of the washcloth. Have the student take and hold a breath, then put the washcloth up to his or her pursed lips (be sure that the side touching the lips is not the soapy side) and blow. Have him or her remove the cloth from the lips to get another breath. Then, the student puts it back to the lips, as before, and blows again. Direct the student to look at the soapy side of the washcloth. He or she has made bubbles appear magically!

# Water *(cont.)*

## Materials:

- small pool, tub, or sensory table filled with water
- containers: cup, pint, quart, gallon
- pitcher
- Liquid Measurement Chart (See page 180.)
- Liquid Measurement Cards (See below.)

## Liquid Measurement

By filling containers and pouring water from one container into another, each child will learn to associate an amount and size with the words cup, pint, quart, and gallon. Children will also begin to experiment with how many of one container will fill another.

Provide measuring cups or containers that are clearly labeled cup, pint, quart, and gallon. Young children can experiment pouring water from one container to the other. Older children can use the containers provided to experiment with how many of one container will fill another container. You may wish to provide the direction cards on page 180 for older children to follow once they have had plenty of time to experiment. Laminate the chart or cards in order to waterproof them. Teacher Note: Introduce the cards in order from the smallest measurement to largest.

**Teacher Note:** Substitute metric measurement containers if appropriate to the curriculum.

# Water *(cont.)*

## Liquid Measurement Chart

Experiment with the measurement cups and water. Try to answer each of the questions.

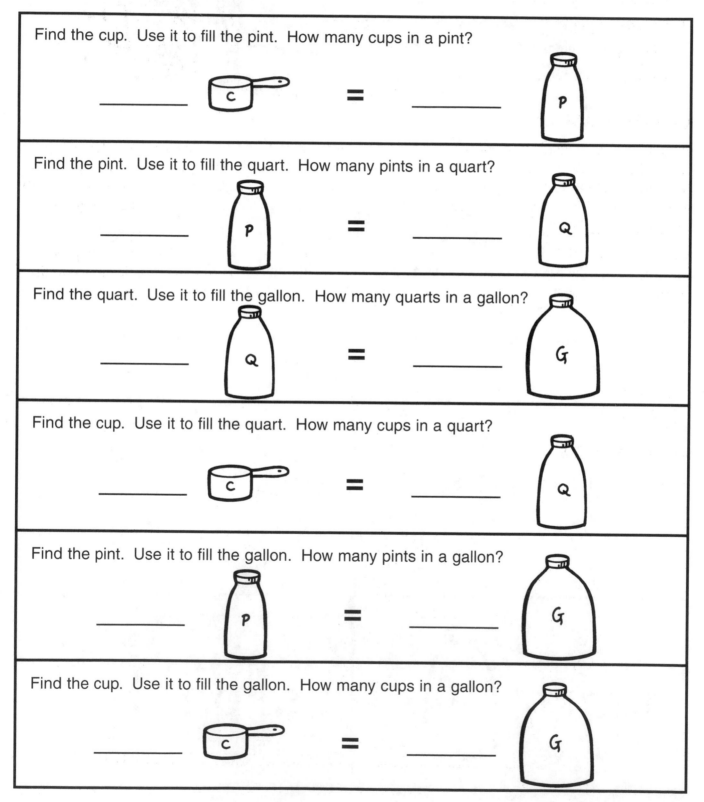

Find the cup. Use it to fill the pint. How many cups in a pint?

_____  C  =  _____  P

Find the pint. Use it to fill the quart. How many pints in a quart?

_____  P  =  _____  Q

Find the quart. Use it to fill the gallon. How many quarts in a gallon?

_____  Q  =  _____  G

Find the cup. Use it to fill the quart. How many cups in a quart?

_____  C  =  _____  Q

Find the pint. Use it to fill the gallon. How many pints in a gallon?

_____  P  =  _____  G

Find the cup. Use it to fill the gallon. How many cups in a gallon?

_____  C  =  _____  G

# Water *(cont.)*

## Materials:

- funnel
- clear plastic pitchers
- food coloring
- clear plastic cups
- water

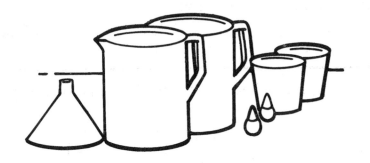

## Colored Water

Help the children make colored water in one pitcher by filling it half full with water and adding a few drops of food coloring. Watch the water's color change as the food coloring permeates the clear water. Next, have a child place the funnel securely in the top of the empty pitcher. Demonstrate how to slowly pour the colored water through the funnel. Once all the water has been poured through, the child will enjoy repeating the process by pouring it back and fourth from the containers.

Make one cup of each color by dropping red, yellow, and blue food coloring in separate, clear plastic cups. Have each student experiment mixing the colors by pouring water from the plastic cups into the larger pitchers. You may want to guide the student to mix different colors during different sessions.

**Session 1:** red and yellow

**Session 2:** yellow and blue

**Session 3:** blue and red

**Session 4:** all the colors together

# Beans and Rice

## Materials:

- sensory table
- sensory table contents (See page 172.)
- scoops
- small bowls

## Mixing Recipes

This activity can be done with almost any of the recommended contents for sensory tables. (See page 172 for sensory table content ideas.)

A few days before you are ready to change the contents of your sensory tables, place some scoops in the sensory tables and have the children make recipes with the contents. Younger children can experiment with mixing the various textures. Older children can actually follow a recipe. Create recipe cards with the directions you want the children to follow. For example, have each student mix a recipe of two scoops of rice and one scoop of beans. Have the student mix the recipe in a smaller bowl.

## Variation

If the contents of the recipe are large enough for the children to manipulate easily, set up a sorting activity. Each student can sort the ingredients back into the original sensory table containers. For example, if you have the student mix a recipe of packing popcorn and bow-tie noodles, he or she can easily manipulate those pieces in order to sort them. If the student mixes beans and sand or salt, the sand/salt can be strained using a sifter or colander.

# Beans and Rice *(cont.)*

## Materials:

- sensory table
- sensory table contents (See page 172 for suggestions.)
- objects to hide (See page 177 for suggestions.)
- small bowls

## Object Hunt

Fill a sensory table with desired contents (e.g., beans). Then, hide objects inside the sensory table contents (e.g., bear counters). Have each student search through the beans in order to locate the bear counters. You may ask the student to locate only the blue bear counters, and place them in a small bowl located near the sensory table. This requires the student to practice sorting skills while using the sensory table.

Make the task of locating the bear counters more difficult by placing a variety of other types of counters in the beans. For example, you could place nuts in the beans along with the bears.

Challenge each student to locate the bear counters with his or her eyes closed. In this way, the student will have to rely on his or her sense of touch to locate the bear counters. Tell the student that he or she can't use hands to find the counters, but may use a strainer or slotted spoon.

# Touch Tables

## Materials:

- sensory table
- lotion
- towel or paper towels

## Lotion Rub

Provide lotion (baby lotion is an excellent choice) for students to use in a sensory table. You can select non-scented lotion or scented lotion for use in this activity. For younger children, squeeze the lotion into the sensory table for the children. For students who are capable, allow them to squeeze the lotion into the table. Encourage each student to rub the lotion on his or her hands and arms in order to feel the slippery texture of lotion. Have the student use his or her fingers and hands to explore the feel of the lotion inside the sensory table. The student can finger paint with the lotion. Older children can practice forming letters, numbers, shapes, or even spelling words in the lotion. For variety in the texture of the lotion, try adding other substances, such as crushed walnuts, glitter, birdseed, and rice. See page 177 for additional ideas of items that could be added to the lotion.

## Safety Note

Be sure to check if any of your students have allergies before using scented lotions.

# Touch Tables *(cont.)*

## Materials:

- sensory table
- shaving cream or finger paint
- tagboard
- smock (1 per child)
- towel  Fs or paper towels

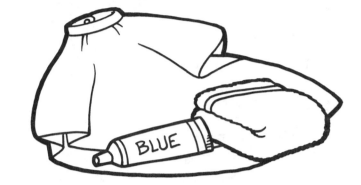

## Finger Painting Fun

Finger painting is always a big hit with young children. Squeeze paint onto the sensory table. Allow each child to experiment with how the paint feels in his or her fingers and how it feels to move it around the sensory table. Young children can explore drawing in the finger paint. Once older children have had sufficient time to experiment, you may wish to provide directions on a piece of tagboard for a skill you would like the children to practice. Program the tagboard with skills for students to practice.

Consider having the children practice some of the following skills:

- making shapes
- forming letters
- forming numbers
- spelling words
- adding or subtracting.

## Helpful Hint

◆ Try using shaving cream in the sensory table to alter the texture the student is touching. Also, cookie sheets or pizza trays make excellent sensory tables for this activity.

## Materials:

- finger paint
- half-gallon plastic, resealable bags

## Less Mess

An equally fun (but less messy) way to do finger painting is to fill several half-gallon plastic, resealable bags with 2–3 tablespoons (30–45 mL) of paint. Seal the bag tightly. Lay the bag on a flat surface. Use your hands to smooth out the paint in the bag. Have each child use his or her finger to practice drawing shapes, and practice writing letters and numbers. It helps to have several bags made up ahead of time so that if a bag gets torn, it can be thrown away and another is readily available.

# Touch Tables *(cont.)*

## Materials:

- shoebox or other box with a lid
- a variety of objects with various textures

## What Do You Feel?

Create a Feelie Box (see page 187) in a shoebox or draw-string bag. Place a variety of objects inside the box for each student to experience with only his or her sense of touch. Put the box in a place where the student can reach into the box without seeing the contents.

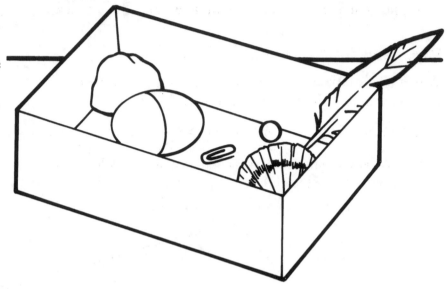

To begin with, place only one object, at a time, in the box. Give the student time to feel the object. Then, have him or her try to guess what the object is. Once the student becomes familiar with how objects feel, place more than one object in the box. Name an object (e.g., a spoon) or a texture (e.g., something soft) for the student to locate in the box. Once the student has found that object, he or she pulls it out of the box to show the group. Allow students to use objects in the room to place in the Feelie Box. Have the students quiz their friends on the contents of the box.

Try some of these objects in a Feelie Box:

| | | |
|---|---|---|
| • beans | • leaves | • rocks |
| • birthday candles | • marbles | • shells |
| • cereal | • netting | • small stuffed animals |
| • cotton balls | • nuts | • small toys |
| • cotton swabs | • oats (dry) | • sponges |
| • crayons | • paper | • stones |
| • fabric swatches | • paper clips | • straw |
| • feathers | • pencils | • sugar |
| • film containers | • pennies | • tongs |
| • flour | • pens | • wood |
| • kitchen utensils | • plastic eggs | • wood shavings |

# Touch Tables *(cont.)*

## Materials:

- a box (about the size of a shoebox)
- a sock
- scissors
- glue gun and glue sticks (or white glue)

## Directions for Making a Feelie Box:

With a Feelie Box, a student can experience objects with only his or her sense of touch. Using a Feelie Box helps to discourage the urge to take a peek.

1. Cut a circle that is approximately 3" (8 cm) in diameter in the side of a shoebox.

2. Cut the toe out of a sock so that you have a tube shape.

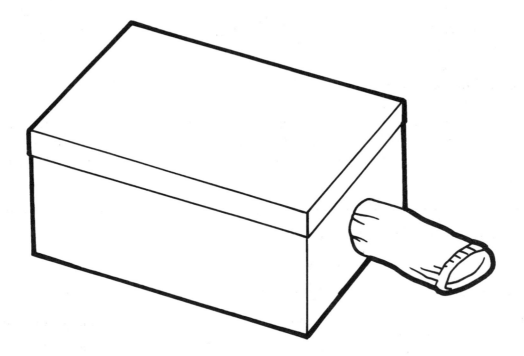

3. Glue one end of the sock on the inside of the shoebox around the edge of the circle that was cut out. (Hot glue works best for this, although white glue will work, too.)

4. Place an object inside the Feelie Box. Cover the shoebox with the lid. A student puts his or her hand through the sock in order to reach inside the Feelie Box.

# Oral Sensory Tables

## Materials:

- sensory table (or a cookie sheet)
- small paper cups or muffin pan
- food samples (See page 189–190 for suggestions.)

## Sample Platter

Providing children with activities that require them to use their sense of taste encourages them to experience the world in yet a different way. Children may balk at trying something new at the dinner table; however, they are usually willing when it comes to a sensory table experience. Although you may not want to provide each sensory table which requires food preparation with a food purchase regularly, once you see the excitement an oral sensory table generates, you will want to provide the experience at least once in a while for variety.

The easiest way to provide oral activities at a sensory table is to place one portion of the food you will be having the students sample in a small paper cup or in a section of a muffin pan. Place enough paper cups for each of your students on a cookie sheet for carrying ease. You may wish to have water available for students to drink afterwards, especially for bitter or sour tasting foods.

Be sure to establish procedures for sampling foods at an oral sensory table. Be sure students know what they should do if they do not like the food.

At an oral sensory table, you may wish to simply provide one or two foods which you think students may not have been exposed to, or you may wish to have students sample several foods, and then label them bitter, sour, sweet, or salty.

Lists of food you may wish to try at an oral sensory table are on pages 189–190. Consider graphing the responses to the different food selections.

## Safety Note

Be sure to find out about student allergies before providing food experiences.

# Oral Sensory Tables (cont.)

## Sample Platter (cont.)

Here are a variety of snacks that can be used at sensory tables. The lists are sorted by color, so you can coordinate serving a colored snack while learning about a certain color.

### Blue
- blue gelatin
- blue gummy snacks
- blueberries

### Red
- apple
- beets
- cherries
- cranberry sauce
- jam
- ketchup
- radishes
- red gelatin
- red grapes
- strawberries
- tomato sauce
- tomato soup
- tomatoes
- watermelon

### Yellow
- appleauce
- bananas
- butter
- buttered toast
- cheese
- crackers
- eggs
- grapefruit
- jam
- lemon ice
- lemonade
- lemons
- pears
- pineapple
- squash
- yellow gelatin

### Orange
- acorn squash
- apricots
- cantaloupe
- carrots
- cheese
- fish crackers
- orange gelatin
- orange juice
- oranges
- peaches
- pumpkin
- unpopped kernels of corn

**Teacher Note:** Food coloring can be added to a variety of foods (such as whipped cream, cream cheese, or mashed potatoes) for color comparisons.

# Oral Sensory Tables *(cont.)*

## Sample Platter *(cont.)*

---

### Purple
- gelatin
- grape jelly
- grape juice
- grapes
- plums

---

### Green
- grapes
- green apple
- green gelatin
- kiwi fruit
- pears

---

### Brown
- apple butter
- apple juice
- banana bread
- carob chips
- chocolate milk
- cinnamon
- gingerbread
- graham crackers
- mushrooms
- peanut butter
- prunes
- raisins
- some cereals
- toast
- whole wheat bread

---

Occasionally, offer some of the following foods for variety and provide new experiences:
- artichokes
- asparagus
- bell peppers
- chow mein noodles
- coconut
- cranberries
- dried fruit
- dried meat
- granola
- mango
- papaya

---

**Teacher Note:** Students will probably have had experience with many of the foods previously listed. Rotate the texture and kind of snack, and the children will never tire of them. Most of all, talk, talk, talk about the aspects of food. This is as important as the nutrition itself.

# Scent Tables

## Materials:

- sensory table (or a cookie sheet)
- cotton balls (unscented)
- extracts (vanilla, coconut, etc.)
- film canisters or small paper cups

## Aroma Table

Place a few drops of extract on a cotton ball. Repeat for as many extracts as you have available. Place each cotton ball in its own film canister (or small cup). Label the bottom with the scent. Place the canisters on a cookie sheet, or in scattered locations around the classroom. Have each student rotate to each of the containers and smell the cotton ball inside. The student tries to guess what scent is on each cotton ball.

You will find (and your students will, too) that some of the extracts stain the cotton balls. Before long your students will be using the color of the stain rather than the scent to identify the aroma of the cotton balls. When this happens, you will want to mix the extracts with a mixture of water and food coloring before placing the drops on the cotton balls. Then, when the student completes this activity, he or she will be forced to use his or her sense of smell.

# Creative Play

Play is how children learn, and should always be a positive time. Play should include children using their five senses whenever possible. Furthermore, play should encourage imagination, creativity, and pretending.

Children discover things themselves through trial and error. As adults, we need to encourage their play, not direct it. Children do most things out of curiosity. Practically everything a child does is play. It can be joyful, serious, solitary, or social. Play is frequent, repetitive, and always creative. Play helps children understand what they see and experience in the real world.

While children are having fun, they acquire, practice, and master skills. They strengthen their small and large muscles and form attitudes toward others and themselves. When children play, they should feel that they are successful. Success promotes a child's self-confidence and increases the desire to do and learn more. Most children go through a sequence (see below) as they learn to play. Play is a primary way to develop motor skills.

### Random and Exploratory Play

This play occurs when a child shakes, moves, bangs, and turns over toys and other objects. A child explores objects by tasting, looking at, listening to, moving, and feeling them with his or her whole body. (To encourage random and exploratory play, give the child opportunities to explore the objects/toys, using different senses. The toys should be safe, nontoxic, and interesting.)

### Early Functional Play

This play occurs when a child begins to use objects the way they were meant to be used. For example, the child will use a brush to brush hair, but he or she will also use the same brush for other things. The child will roll a ball, stack blocks, listen to a toy phone, and use a washcloth to wash things.

### Later Functional Play

This type of play occurs when a child uses most toys and objects appropriately. The child will be able to respond to the request, "Show me what goes on your foot," by picking up the shoe or pointing to a picture of a shoe.

### Creative-Symbolic Play

Creative-symbolic play happens when a child begins to use symbols in play such as pretending that a box is a train or a hairbrush is a telephone.

### Imaginative Play

Imaginative play happens when the child uses increased creativity and imagination in play. The child may play with imaginary friends or pretend to be someone else. The child will act out familiar household routines when playing "house." This section provides a variety of ideas you can use in your classroom to engage and encourage children in play.

# Painting Activities

## Materials:

- empty containers

- paintbrushes

- water

## Water Painting

Painting with water is an activity that can provide hours of good, clean fun. It is easy and it can be done anywhere you have a stretch of cement, sidewalk, fence, or a wall.

Find an outdoor space for the children to work. Fill an empty container or bucket with water. Demonstrate how to dip a paint brush and paint with the water. The water will make a nice painted surface, and children will be able to see the areas they have already painted. On a hot day, the painted area will dry very quickly. Some children think it is magic!

Encourage children to make designs, draw shapes, write letters and numbers, practice spelling words, and explore all of the different things that can be done with the water paint. Be prepared for children to get wet. This is a great activity to do on a very hot day.

As an alternative, use paint rollers instead of brushes. Rollers often encourage children to use a full range of arm motions. Encourage them to reach as high as they can, on tiptoes, when painting walls.

# Painting Activities *(cont.)*

## Materials:

- butcher paper
- tree branches
- tempera paint (watered-down)
- paint container
- cover-ups (old shirts or large T-shirts)

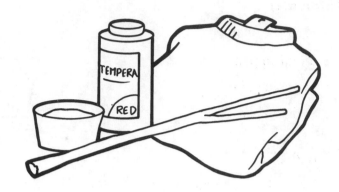

## Branch Painting

You will want to do this activity outside. Hang a large piece of butcher paper on a wall. Hang the paper low enough for students to reach, yet high enough so that students will have to use their shoulders to reach to the upper portions of the paper. Collect a variety of sizes of leafy branches. (Pepper tree branches work well.) Fill a container that has a large opening (such as a small tub or roasting pan) with paint. A student lays the branch in the paint, then uses the branch to swat paint on the piece of butcher paper. The motion used is more of an "overhead" swatting motion than applying brush strokes. Encourage the student to use overhand motions.

# Painting Activities *(cont.)*

## Materials:

- yarn
- a muffin pan
- tempera paint
- white paper

## Yarn Art

Cut pieces of yarn about 12" (30 cm) long. Place a variety of colors of paint in the various sections of an old muffin pan. Use one piece of yarn for each color of paint. Have a student dip the yarn into the paint and drag the yarn (with paint on it) over a sheet of white paper that has been taped to a table surface. Use a variety of colors and thicknesses of yarn to create a unique picture. You may want to limit the number of colors that a student has to work with in order to avoid a muddy look that often occurs when too many colors are used.

An alternative is to fold a sheet of paper in half. Open the paper up and lay it on the table. Dip the yarn into the paint, then lay the yarn in a design on only half of the paper. Be sure to have one end of the yarn so that it drapes off of the paper. Fold the paper in half again (with the yarn still inside). Then, while holding the paper in place with one hand, use the other hand to pull gently on the end of the yarn that is sticking out of the folded paper. Pull until the piece of yarn is completely out of the folded paper. Open the piece of paper to reveal the symmetrical design. This makes a beautiful card or wrapping paper.

# Painting Activities *(cont.)*

## Materials:

- a plastic tub
- tempera paint (watered-down)
- marbles
- white construction paper

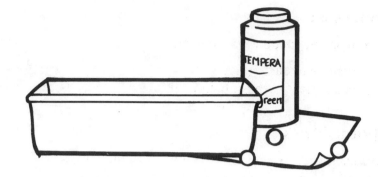

## Marble Painting

Place a sheet of white construction paper in the basin of a plastic tub. Add a small amount of watered-down tempera paint onto the paper (about the size of a quarter). Place a marble inside the tub. In order to create a picture, a student holds the tub with both hands and rolls the marble around inside the tub. The result is a beautiful and unique art project. You may choose to add two or three colors of paint to the tub; however, limit the total amount of paint so that the paper does not become too wet.

Long boxes that are used for rolls of paper are great for two-person marble painting. Have each student stand at one end of the long box and move it up and down to make the box move.

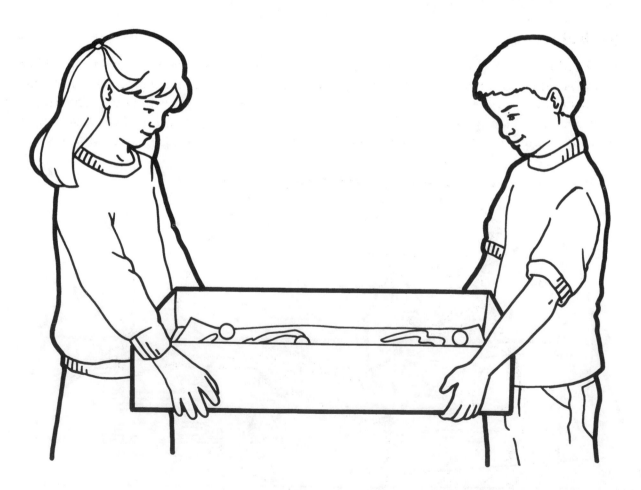

# Play Activities

## Materials:

- wooden spoon (1 per child)
- objects to carry (e.g., beanbags, marbles, balls)

## Spoon Walk

Give each child a wooden spoon with a long handle. Have the child practice walking around while carrying an object in the bowl of the spoon. Begin with stable objects such as beanbags. As the child's skills improve, change the object to small balls or marbles. If carrying the spoon by the handle is difficult for the child, have him or her grasp the handle closer to the bowl of the spoon. As stability increases, have the child move his or her hands back farther on the handle.

## Materials:

- objects to carry (20 per team)
- empty bowl (1 per team)
- wooden spoon (1 per team)

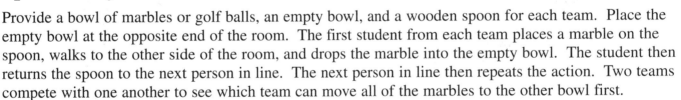

## Spoon Relay

Provide a bowl of marbles or golf balls, an empty bowl, and a wooden spoon for each team. Place the empty bowl at the opposite end of the room. The first student from each team places a marble on the spoon, walks to the other side of the room, and drops the marble into the empty bowl. The student then returns the spoon to the next person in line. The next person in line then repeats the action. Two teams compete with one another to see which team can move all of the marbles to the other bowl first.

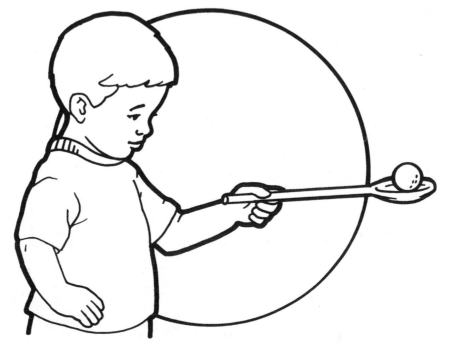

# Play Activities *(cont.)*

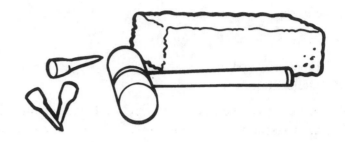

## Materials:

- golf tees (20 per child)
- a wooden mallet (1 per child)
- a piece of Styrofoam (1 per child)

## Hammering Nails

Locate pieces of Styrofoam or purchase them; Styrofoam can be found at your local craft store. If you purchase the Styrofoam, buy blocks that are at least 3" (8 cm) thick. You don't have to purchase Styrofoam. It comes in mail-order packages, as well as in boxes in order to protect large items such as TVs, computers, radios, etc.

Provide 20 golf tees, a wooden mallet, and a piece of Styrofoam for each student. Have the student hold the "nail" (the golf tee) carefully and gently tap it with the wooden mallet until it is embedded in the Styrofoam. As the student becomes used to tapping the golf tees into the Styrofoam, encourage him or her to create a design or pattern.

A real hammer, nails, and soft wood may be used if working in a small group situation where students can be closely monitored.

## Materials:

- same-colored golf tees or nails (10 per child)
- hammer (1 per child)

## Hammer and Count

Dedicate a dirt area of the play yard for hammering. Have an adult supervise this area when children are using it. The adult hands a child 10 nails or golf tees and a hammer. If you use golf tees, hand each child 10 same-colored tees. If you use nails, spray paint the nails in order to color-code them.

The child hammers the nails into the dirt. When he or she is finished, the child uses the claw part of the hammer in order to pull the nails back out of the dirt. Once all 10 nails have been successfully located and pulled out, the child hands them back to the supervising adult. The child can then hammer 10 different-colored nails into the dirt or do another activity. This process provides counting practice for the child, as well as ensures that no nails get lost in the dirt creating a safety hazard.

In addition, you may wish to try having students hammer bottle caps into the dirt.

# Play Activities *(cont.)*

## Materials:

- none

## Pantomime

Children are very excited when they are first introduced to pantomime. Pantomime allows for creativity and the use of the imagination. If the pantomime activities are selected carefully, they help develop shoulder strength and control. Choose one student to be the actor. The remaining students can guess what activity is being acted out. Once the action has been correctly guessed, give each of the remaining children a chance to act out an activity.

Have students pretend to:

- shoot an arrow

- put on an apron

- put on a coat

- put on gloves

- play the guitar

- scoop ice cream

- climb up and down a ladder

- paddle downstream

- chop down a tree with an ax

- build a building with blocks

- dig a big hole with a shovel

- wrap a gift

- hammer a nail into the wall and hang a picture

- put a key in a treasure chest and open it

- hang up laundry on a clothesline

- put on overalls

# Play Activities *(cont.)*

## Vertical Activities

Having students do any activity that is vertical is excellent for gross motor skill development. Vertical activities require children to use a range of motions with their arms that help them gain strength and control of the arm muscles. Consider changing almost any activity you do on a horizontal surface by simply providing a vertical surface for the children to use.

Consider the following vertical surfaces:

◆ chalkboard or blackboard

◆ an easel

◆ a desk or table turned on its side

◆ a wall

◆ the side of a filing cabinet or bookcase

◆ a closet door (one that will not be opened!)

## Vertical Games

Have students play games that have stands that create vertical surfaces. Have each student play the game while lying on his or her stomach. This requires the student to use a lot of arm movement to play the game. If the student is not able, place the game on a table until arm strength is further developed.

### Materials:

• play dough (See pages 238–239 for recipes.)

• a vertical surface (See ideas above.)

## Play Dough

Define a vertical workspace for the children. Provide each student with play dough. Have the student pat the play dough flat like a pancake on the vertical surface. Then he or she can try using cookie cutters or creating snakes. The student can try almost any play dough activity, but on a vertical surface.

# Play Activities *(cont.)*

## Vertical Activities *(cont.)*
### Materials:

- tape
- paper
- crayons or colored pencils
- a vertical surface (See page 200.)

## Two-Handed Drawing

Tape a large piece of paper on a vertical surface. Have each student use both hands to draw shapes on the piece of paper. Have him or her begin with simple shapes, such as straight lines or circles. Then, the student can gradually increase the complexity of the shapes to triangles, squares, letters, and numbers. Drawing with the non-dominant hand will be difficult for the student to do. Don't worry, the idea is not to make the student ambidextrous, but to provide an activity that will require the student to practice moving both arms. You may need to explain to students that most people have a dominant hand, but that they will be using both hands for this activity.

### Materials:

- tape
- paper
- stickers
- crayons or colored pencils
- a vertical surface (See page 200.)

## Drawing Vertically

Tape a piece of paper on a vertical surface. Have each student create a picture using crayons or colored pencils. Provide the student with stickers if desired. Have the student place the stickers on the paper, then draw a scene around the stickers.

The student can paint a picture on a vertical surface, too. An ideal vertical surface for this is a paint easel; however, if you do not have an easel, simply tape a piece of paper on any vertical surface. You may want to cover the surface below, as paint tends to drip.

If the vertical surface happens to be a textured wall or shingles, the student may enjoy doing rubbings using the long side of the crayons. Encourage him or her to reach as high as possible and come straight down with the crayon.

# Play Activities *(cont.)*

## Vertical Activities *(cont.)*

## Materials:

- chalk

- blackboard

- construction paper

## O's on a Bumpy Road

Having students work on a blackboard is an excellent way to promote movement of the shoulders and arms. Because blackboards are usually mounted on the wall at a level appropriate for an adult, students will have to use their arms to reach for the board.

Draw a wavy line on the blackboard. Place a sheet of construction paper or carpet square on the floor at the middle point of the blackboard. One at a time, have each student stand on the paper facing the chalkboard. The child remains on the paper while completing this activity. Starting at the left side of the line, he or she draws O's on top of the line. The child continues until the end of the line is reached. When the child has finished, have him or her draw O's under the line.

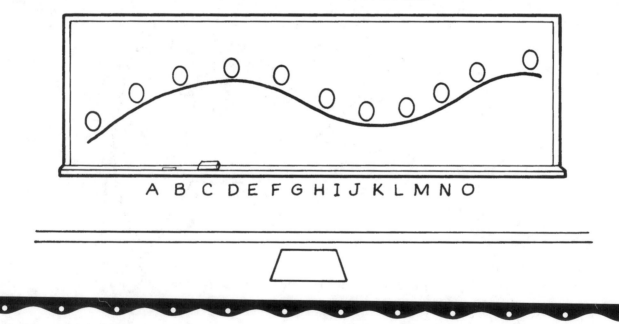

## Variations

Of course, a student can write any letter on the Bumpy Road. Have the student practice writing the current letter of study (or current shape). The idea is to have the student use the full range of movement of the arms and shoulders.

Make the wavy line higher on the blackboard. This will require the student to reach when writing the letter. It is okay for the student to stand on his or her tiptoes in order to reach the top of the line.

# Play Activities *(cont.)*

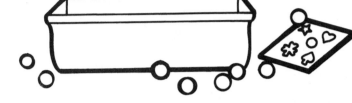

## Materials:

- a plastic container (e.g., a washing tub)
- stickers
- marbles

## Marble Roll

Locate a container that students can easily hold in their hands. Place stickers with the numbers 1–5 in the basin of the tub. Place a marble (a washer or magnet will also work) inside the tub. Have each student hold the tub in his or her hands and roll the marble around the basin of the tub to each of the stickers in the correct order. You may choose to use letters printed on the stickers or small stickers with a variety of characters on them. Then, you can call out the type of sticker that you want the student to roll the marble on.

# Play Activities *(cont.)*

## Materials:

- fishing poles (See page 205.)
- fish patterns (See page 205.)
- blue yarn or a large piece of blue fabric

## Going Fishing

Create a pond by shaping a piece of blue yarn into a circle on the floor. Make a fishing game using the programmed fish based on a skill on which you are working (see suggestions below). (You may want to laminate the fish for durability.) Slide a paper clip onto each fish; then place the fish in the pond. A student catches all of the fish on his or her pole (the magnet attracts the paper clip). Then he or she works in a small group to match the fish in one of the ways below. Try these two variations of Going Fishing to spark student interest:

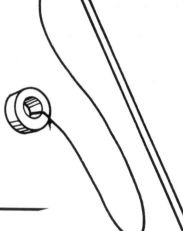

- Use a small (blow-up) swimming pool as your pond.
- Build a fishing booth. Locate a large box (e.g., an appliance box). Cut a back door through which students can enter the booth. Cut a window in the front of the box. Place the pond with fish in it on the outside of the booth. Place a chair or stool on the inside of the booth. A student may sit on the chair in the booth while fishing.

Try having students fish for:

**Color words**—Students match fish with the same color word.

**Colors**—Assign each child a different color fish to find.

**Compound words**—Write one word on each fish. Students match two words that can be placed together to form a compound word.

**Contractions**—Write a contraction on one fish and the words that make up the contraction on two other fish. Students match a contraction to the two words that make up the contraction. (Consider having two "ponds" for this activity.)

**Counting match**—Write numbers on some fish and dots on other fish. Students match each fish with dots on it to the fish with the corresponding number.

**Sequencing numbers**—Students arrange numbers in sequential order.

**Sight words**—Students catch a sight word; then try to read it.

# Play Activities *(cont.)*

### Materials:

- ½" dowel rod, 18" (46 cm) in length
- a magnet
- string
- a stapler

## Directions for Making a Fishing Pole

Staple a piece of string that is about 2' (61 cm) long to one of the ends of a dowel. Tie a doughnut-hole magnet at the end of the string.

### Materials:

- construction paper
- a paper clip

## Directions for Making a Paper Fish

Reproduce the fish pattern below on construction paper. Cut out and laminate each fish. Label each fish (using a permanent marker) with the skill you want children to practice. Attach a paper clip near the mouth of the fish.

# Play Activities *(cont.)*

## Materials:

- chalk
- socks (2 per child)
- a carpet square (1 per child)

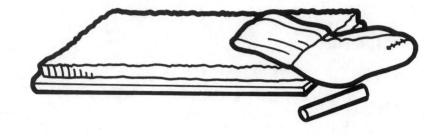

## Sock Erasers

Draw several large figures on the carpet squares using chalk. For younger children, draw shapes, letters, and numbers. For older children, you may want to write spelling words or number sentences on the carpet.

Have each student take his or her shoes off. You can have the student do this activity in his or her own socks; however, you may like to provide some "chalk socks" for the student to wear over the socks so that the student does not get his or her own socks dirty.

Have the student erase the chalk figure on the carpet square with his or her socks. The student moves around the figure in order to erase all of the chalk. Once he or she becomes more skilled at the activity, challenge him or her to stand in one spot while erasing the figure. If you are going to have the student stand in one spot, be sure to draw an appropriately-sized figure so that he or she can reach the entire figure while standing in one place.

# Play Activities *(cont.)*

## Materials:

- Ping-Pong ball (1 per student)
- masking tape

## Line-to-Line

Mark off two lines with masking tape that are approximately 10' (3 m) apart. Place the Ping-Pong ball on one of the lines. Have each student lie down on the floor (with his or her stomach on the floor). The student blows the Ping-Pong ball across the floor until it reaches the other line. He or she moves his or her body closer to the ball in order to blow it again; however, he or she must crawl along the floor using the arms. This activity can be done with a feather, or a wadded-up piece of paper. Once the students are familiar with the activity, play a game such as Ping-Pong Soccer or make an Obstacle Course (as deseribed below).

## Materials:

- Ping-Pong ball (1 per student)
- masking tape

## Ping-Pong Soccer

Create the masking tape lines as mentioned above. One student defends one line and the other student defends the other line. Each student tries to blow the Ping-Pong ball across to the opposing side. If the ball crosses the other line, the student who blew the ball across scores. Keep track of the score and play to a predetermined number of points.

## Materials:

- Ping-Pong ball (1 per student)
- obstacles (e.g., chairs, desks, tunnels, etc.)

## Obstacle Course

Create an obstacle course for each student to maneuver a Ping-Pong ball through while using the same technique described in Line-to-Line. Have the student blow his or her ball around chairs, under desks, through tunnels, and over hills.

# Play Activities *(cont.)*

## Materials:

- baster or eye dropper
- containers
- water

## Water Transfer

Fill one container with water. Place an empty container next to the container filled with water. A student must use a baster (or eye dropper) to gather water from the water container, move to the empty container, and then squeeze the baster until empty, then repeat the action. The student will have to maintain the suction on the baster to successfully transfer the water.

As the student becomes skilled at maintaining the suction, move the empty container farther away from the container filled with water. See how far apart you can move the containers and still have him or her maintain the suction.

Have the student try different locomotor skills while trying to transfer the water. For example, have him or her fill the baster with water and hop over to the empty container. It will be more difficult for the student to maintain the suction while in motion.

Create a relay using the same technique. Two teams can compete against one another to see which team can fill the empty container first.

# Dramatic Play Activities

## Materials:

- varies based on theme (see below)

## Dramatic Play

Set aside an area of your classroom for dramatic play. Dramatic play is very important to young children. It nurtures a variety of skills while bringing them tremendous pleasure and countless hours of imagination. By varying the objects in a dramatic play area, students can move in a variety of different ways, using both gross and fine motor skills in order to use the objects. It is important to change the dramatic play area when the children appear to have lost interest in the materials. Children will not play appropriately in the area when they are no longer stimulated. By adding new props to the area, interest is renewed.

## Theme Boxes

Over time, a teacher can gather props to make theme boxes for the dramatic-play area. Use your imagination and develop your own theme boxes to use inside and outside. Simply begin to save everything! You never know when it will come in handy. Theme box ideas include the following:

**Office Workers:** pads of paper, typewriter, pencil holders, pens and pencils, stamps (music club and book club stamps that come in the mail work well), stapler, tape, envelopes, hole punchers, old keyboards and computers, and pictures of office workers

**Flower Shop:** flower and garden magazines, small garden tools, garden hats, gloves, aprons, plastic, silk and tissue-paper flowers, vases, Styrofoam squares, baskets, cash register, play money, and pictures of flowers

**Beach Party:** beach towels, sunglasses, hats, empty suntan lotion bottles, small portable radio, plastic fish, fish net, fishing pole, inner tubes, umbrellas, beach balls, picnic basket, picnic blanket, plastic food, and pictures of the beach and ocean

# Dramatic Play Activities *(cont.)*

## Theme Boxes *(cont.)*

**Veterinarian Office:** small stuffed animals, small rolls of cloth bandages, adhesive tape, cotton balls, stethoscope, disposable masks, magnifying glass, pet comb and brush, thermometer, pet travel boxes, old cages, and pictures of animals

**Beauty Shop:** smocks, snap-in curlers, hand-held hairdryers (with cords cut off), towels, curling irons (with cords cut off), hair pins, hair clips, empty spray bottles, empty shampoo bottles, mirrors, ribbons, bows, a telephone, and pictures of hairstyles. (**Safety Note:** Do not include combs or hair brushes.)

**Sporting Goods Store:** backpacks, heavy socks, helmets, baseball caps, gloves, shoes, various types of balls, headbands, tennis rackets, goggles, ski caps, scuba diving fins, snorkels, hand-held weights, and pictures of athletes

**Camping:** plastic bugs, wood for fire, water bottles, pillows, fly swatter, small tent, frying pan, spatula, sunglasses, small cooler, flashlight, grill, paper plates, utensils, sleeping bags, binoculars, fishing poles, coffee pot, plastic food, and pictures of outdoor scenes

Other theme box ideas include: a bakery, gas station, repair shop, hardware store, grocery store, fast-food restaurant, doctor/nurse office, police station, fire station, post office, dentist office, pizza parlor, and ice-cream store.

# Dramatic Play Activities *(cont.)*

Theme boxes can be used for outside play as well. Put together outdoor boxes such as these:

**Pipes:** PVC pipes and elbows to be used in sand and water areas

**Hoops:** plastic hula hoops to jump in, roll around, crawl through, and more

**Painting:** painting items like buckets, aprons, several brushes in various sizes, water, paint, chalk, dish soap, and paper

**Squirting:** various squirt bottles

**Digging:** buckets, shovels, pots, and pans

**Transportation:** cars, trains, and trucks

**Gardening:** outdoor gardening supplies including: watering cans, small hoses, small rakes, child-size gardening tools, gloves, kneepads, and hats

**Habitats:** large and small blocks, toy cars and trucks, and plastic animals and people.

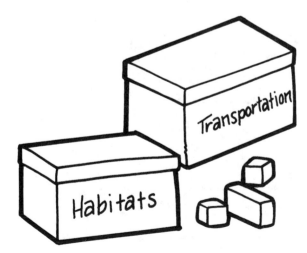

# Cooking Activities

Whether we realize it or not, cooking requires a lot of movement. Stirring, mixing, shaking, and pouring are all activities which require shoulder, wrist, hand, and finger stability. Having children help create recipes is an excellent way to involve students in both fine and gross motor movement. And, best of all, they get to sample yummy food when finished!

Here are some easy recipes that involve children in the snack time experience. You can easily use these recipes to coincide with your weekly theme.

**Ingredients:**
bananas (½ banana per child)
small craft sticks
small jar of honey
small bowl of toasted wheat germ
crushed nuts
peanut butter
dry powered milk

## Directions for Making Frozen Bananas

Beforehand, cut bananas in half and put a craft stick in the cut end for a handle. Place the bananas in the freezer. After the bananas are frozen, the children can help roll the bananas in honey, wheat germ, and nuts. Other toppings include peanut butter and dry milk. Smear on frozen bananas. **Teacher Note:** Children can put on gloves and do this activity with little help.

**Ingredients:**
1 cup (240 mL) cottage cheese
½ cup (120 mL) sour cream
1 cup (240 mL) mayonnaise
½ tsp. (2.5 mL) Worcestershire sauce
salt and pepper to taste
carrot sticks
celery sticks
raw broccoli (cut)
raw cherry tomatoes (cut)

## Directions for Making Vegetable Dip

Place cottage cheese in a mixing bowl. Add sour cream. Beat with wire whisk so that each child gets a turn stirring. Add remaining ingredients (except the vegetables) and stir.

## Safety Note

Remember to have the children wash their hands before preparing any foods, and be sure to find out about student allergies before providing food experiences.

# Cooking Activities *(cont.)*

**Ingredients:**

one bottle corn syrup or 2 cups (480 mL) honey

one 18 oz. (500 g) jar peanut butter

one small box instant dry milk

one box confectioner's sugar

waxed paper

## Directions for Making Peanut Butter Play Dough

Mix the ingredients together and give each child a piece of wax paper for a placemat. Let him or her roll the dough and eat it.

**Ingredients:**

one cup (240 mL) each O-shaped cereal, corn-rice cereal, fruit-flavored O-shaped cereal, and pretzel sticks

one cup (240 mL) raisins

one cup (240 mL) yogurt-covered raisins

one cup (240 mL) chocolate chips

one cup (240 mL) mini candy-coated chocolate pieces

one box small snack baggies

## Directions for Making Bird Seed

This is a great activity to practice pouring and scooping. Each child can take a turn pouring one cup (240 mL) of ingredients into a very large bowl. Stir. Give the child a baggie and let him or her practice scooping the mixture with a large spoon into the baggie. Eat and enjoy.

**Ingredients:**

two 8 oz. (225 kg) packages softened cream cheese

one small can drained, unsweetened, crushed pineapple

$\frac{1}{8}$ cup (30 mL) milk

spoons

crackers

## Directions for Making Cream Cheese and Pineapple Dip

Mix ingredients. Add milk to make an easy-spreading consistency. Give each child a spoon and a cracker. Let the child practice spooning skills by allowing him or her to scoop the cream cheese mix onto his or her own cracker.

# Music Activities

Music plays an important role in the lives of young children. Babies are rocked to sleep with lullabies. A toddler's constant motion is often accompanied by songs and changes of his or her own creation. Preschoolers enjoy creating their own soundmakers and are fascinated with the sounds they make.

Music includes singing, moving, listening, playing instruments, and creating music. Songs foster language development, social skills, rhythm, coordination, listening skills; they are used as an outlet for feelings and ideas.

Music improves auditory discrimination, voice quality, memory, and sequencing skills, and it increases vocabulary while allowing the child to be an active learner; It can be used to teach many concepts and skills, including math, phonics, colors, shapes, feelings; and language concepts such as fast and slow, high and low, loud and soft, and more. Music also helps children to interpret and understand signals and cues they hear.

Researchers are finding that music can boost the brain power of children. They have discovered that when young children are exposed to singing, playing instruments, and listening to classical or other complex music, they have higher spatial and temporal intelligence test scores and their ability for mathematical reasoning is increased. Classical music helps to develop speech, movement abilities, and left-brain thinking skills.

## "The Mozart Effect"

Dr. Alfred Tomatis, a French physician, believes that Mozart's music prepares the mind and body for learning, creativity, and rest. He asserts that even in the womb (after five months), babies are aware of high sound frequencies. Certain melodies (frequencies) help to stimulate the language centers of the brain, and the music by Mozart gives the healthiest of sounds. Mozart's music is simple, clear, organized, efficient, not overly emotional, and easy to listen to while being relaxing and inspiring. Dr. Tomatis recommends playing Mozart in the classroom as background music, emphasizing never to play the music too loudly and no longer than 25 minutes at a time. (Anything over 25 minutes reduces the effectiveness of the music.) You can read more about Mozart's music in Don Campbell's book, *The Mozart Effect*.

# Music Activities *(cont.)*

## Musical Instruments and Aids

Following is a list of instruments and sound makers as well as directions for making them. All of these are worthwhile to have in a preschool classroom.

- records, tapes, and compact discs
- songbooks
- fingerplays
- instruments: rhythm sticks, shakers, and tambourines (directions below); maracas, kazoos, and drums (page 216); and hummer flutes (page 217)
- record, tape, and/or compact disc players
- song cards (See page 217.)
- chants

---

### Materials:

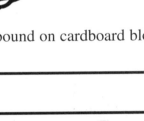

- paper bag
- tape

### Directions for Making a Rhythm Stick

Roll the bag into a tight cylinder. Tape securely. Use the stick to pound on cardboard blocks or furniture to make drumming sounds.

---

### Materials:

- uncooked rice or beans
- 2 paper cups (or 2 small or large plates or a lunch bag)
- tape or a stapler

### Directions for Making a Shaker

Put rice or beans inside two cups or plates tightly taped at the rim (or inside a lunch bag taped shut). Shake. Cylindrical potato chip containers and yogurt containers with plastic lids work well, too.

---

### Materials:

- 2 paper plates or foil pans
- crayons
- dried beans
- masking tape or glue

### Directions for Making a Tambourine

Decorate the plates (or pie tins) with the crayons. Put a handful of beans on the plate. Lay the other plate over the top of the first plate, and tape around the sides so that the beans will not fall out. Shake and bang to music.

---

# Music Activities *(cont.)*

## Musical Instruments and Aids *(cont.)*

### Materials:

- small juice can or cardboard tube
- tinfoil or construction paper
- macaroni (dry)
- rubber band
- ribbons or crepe paper (optional)

### Directions for Making a Maraca

Cover one end of the can with foil or paper. Secure with a rubber band. Fill the tube with macaroni. Cover the end as before. Decorate with ribbon or crepe paper streamers if desired.

### Materials:

- comb
- waxed paper or tissue paper

### Directions for Making a Comb Kazoo

Fold the paper over the comb. Put your lips over the fold and hum a tune, moving the comb from side to side. Throw away the paper after each use, and rinse the comb in warm water and antibacterial soap.

### Materials:

- empty coffee can (or oatmeal carton) with plastic lid
- masking tape
- unsharpened pencils with erasers or sticks
- paper
- crayons
- glue
- glitter
- yarn or string

### Directions for Making a Drum

Glue the lid to the can or carton. Decorate the paper with crayons, glue, and glitter to cover the can. Affix with tape or yarn. Cut a piece of yarn to the necessary length to allow the drum to hang comfortably around the child's neck. Use sticks or unsharpened pencils for drumsticks.

**Safety Note:** Be cautious, never allowing the children to play with these alone. The strings around their necks could be dangerous if left unattended.

# Music Activities *(cont.)*

## Musical Instruments and Aids *(cont.)*

### Materials:

- cardboard tube from paper-towel or toilet-paper roll
- tissue paper
- tape or rubber band
- pencil

### Directions for Making a Hummer Flute

Use the pencil to punch three or four holes in the tube. Cover one end of the tube with a small piece of tissue and secure it with tape or a rubber band. Hum a tune, in the end without the paper, and put your fingers over the holes.

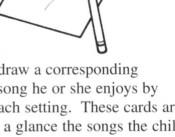

### Materials:

- paper or tagboard
- writing instrument
- songbooks

### Directions for Making a Song Card

Make one card for each song. Write the words on the card and draw a corresponding illustration. This allows the nonverbal or young child to pick a song he or she enjoys by associating it with a picture. The size of the card can vary for each setting. These cards are especially helpful for substitute teachers since they will know at a glance the songs the children enjoy, as well as the words to the songs.

Here is a card example. To make a card for "The Wheels on the Bus," trace a picture of a bus on one side of the card. On the reverse side, print the words to the song. Consider charting some of these favorites on the song cards you make. Sing any of the following nursery rhymes to the tune of *"Ninety-Nine Bottles of Pop on the Wall."*

- Hey Diddle Diddle
- Jack and Jill
- Little Bo Peep
- Old Mother Hubbard
- Hickory Dickory Dock
- Little Boy Blue
- Little Miss Muffet
- Peter, Peter, Pumpkin Eater
- Humpty Dumpty
- Little Jack Horner
- Old King Cole
- Mary, Mary, Quite Contrary

# Games, Obstacles, and Relays

This section provides ideas for combining motor skills in order to play games, create obstacle courses, and have relay races. These three types of activities offer an excellent opportunity for growth and learning. Good sportsmanship, fairness, taking turns, and a number of other personal and social values can be taught through the use of games, obstacle courses, and relay races. As a leader of these games, you have the opportunity to provide guidance and supervision to see that all of the children are included and get the most out of their experiences.

Help the children learn the following skills:

- the importance of cooperation

- to improve decision-making skills in situations that require quick thinking

- to take turns and be patient

- to accept and follow rules

- to accept winning and losing gracefully

- to enjoy physical fitness

## Hints:

◆ The game pages can be photocopied onto thick paper or cardstock and laminated. These can be stored in a file box for easy access. Whenever you are in need of a game, you or your students can refer to the file for ideas. These game cards can be used year after year.

◆ Many of the activities described in the other sections of the book can be altered in order to create a game, obstacle course, or relay. Be creative to alter activities that students enjoy in order to create a game, obstacle course, or relay.

◆ Read page 18 in the introduction of this book titled "Helpful Hints." Many of the hints listed are especially crucial when playing games.

# Games

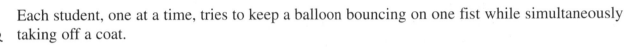

## Materials:

- balloons
- a paper cup of water (1 per child)
- 20 toothpicks
- a large coat

## Balloon Games

Try some of the following balloon games:

Each student, one at a time, tries to keep a balloon bouncing on one fist while simultaneously taking off a coat.

Have the student bounce the balloon while he or she picks up 20 toothpicks, one at a time.

Direct the student to bounce the balloon while drinking a glass of water.

Or, have the student do a more difficult task while bouncing the balloon.

# Games *(cont.)*

## Materials:

- none

## Let's Shake on It

Secretly assign each student a number from 1 to 10. Make sure that each student will have a partner in the large group. Explain to each student that he or she must find his or her partner without speaking. The game begins by having the students scattered around the play area. Each student walks up to another student. Students stick out their hands to shake. One student shakes the other student's hand the same number of times as the number that has been assigned. If the student does not respond with the same number of shakes (because he or she was assigned a different number), he or she continues shaking hands with other students until finding a partner who was assigned the same number. When partners find each other, they link arms and continue to walk safely around the play area until all students have found their partners.

# Games *(cont.)*

## Materials:

- a rubber ball

- a bowling pin
  (or an empty water bottle filled with sand)

## Guard the Pin

Divide the children into groups of five. Have each group form a circle. Place a bowling pin in the middle of the circle. Choose one child to be in the center of each circle. The child in the center tries to guard the pin while the rest of the children in that circle try to knock it down with a ball. The child who knocks down the pin will be in the center for the next game.

# Games *(cont.)*

## Materials:

- a ball

## Brooklyn Bridge

Divide the students into two teams. Line up the teams, facing each other, about 15' (4.5 m) apart. Each student should stand with his or her feet spread far enough apart to allow a ball to pass through. Each team takes a turn at trying to roll the ball through the legs of the opposing team. These students are not allowed to move or to try to stop the ball. If the ball passes through someone's legs, that student is eliminated from the game. The last team with a student still standing is the winner. This game can be played for points, instead of elimination.

# Games *(cont.)*

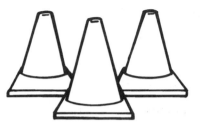

## Materials:

- sponge ball
- rope or cones (to mark goal lines)

## Octopus

Mark the playing field with a goal line at each end. Choose one child to be the octopus; the rest of the students are fish. The object of the game is for the octopus to catch the fish by tagging or hitting them with a sponge ball. If a fish is hit or tagged, he or she becomes frozen in place and is now an octopus tentacle. The tentacles may help the octopus by using their outstretched hands to tag fish. Only the octopus may move around; each tentacle must stay in the same spot where he or she was caught.

To begin play, all the fish line up at one goal line. The octopus calls out, "Fish, fish, swim in my ocean." At this command, the fish must "swim" (hop, walk, run, or any movement agreed upon before the game) across the ocean to the opposite goal. Play continues until all but one fish has been caught. The last fish becomes the octopus in the next game.

# Games *(cont.)*

## Materials:

- a volleyball or utility ball
- a rope or net

## Newcomb

Newcomb is similar to volleyball. The ball is thrown and caught, instead of being hit as in volleyball. Set up a similar court area, taking into consideration the students' ages and available space. Divide the players into two teams, and place them on opposite sides of the rope or net. Flip a coin to see which team will go first. Any player from the first team throws the ball over the net, hoping it will hit the ground before it is caught. If it does, the serving team scores a point. If it is caught, the ball remains in play until it finally falls to the ground. If it falls on the serving team's side, the next serve goes to the other side. If the ball hits the net, goes under the net, or goes out of bounds without anyone touching it, the other team gets to serve. The first team to score at least 21 points, and lead by at least two points, is the winner.

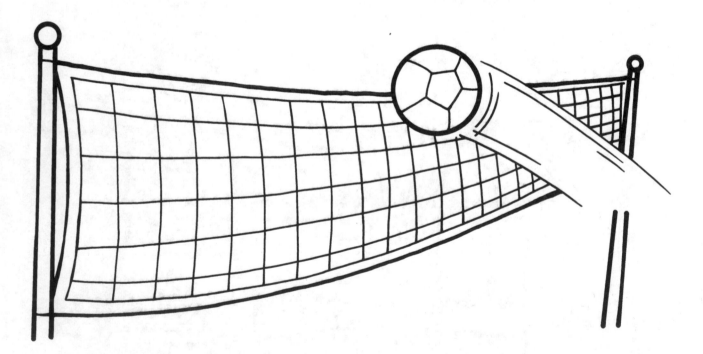

# Games *(cont.)*

## Materials:

- a Ping-Pong ball
- newspaper sheets

## Blizzard

Divide the children into two teams of two or three. Mark off a playing area (table) with a goal line at each end. Have each player make a fan out of a newspaper sheet (see directions below). Place the Ping-Pong ball in the center of the playing area. Each team tries to fan the ball toward the other team's goal without letting the fan touch the ball. If a team gets the ball across its opponent's goal line, the team scores a point. Play continues for a predetermined length of time, or to a certain number of points.

## Materials:

8½" x 11" (8 cm x 13 cm) piece of newspaper

## Directions for Making a Fan

Fold the bottom edge of the paper up 1" (2.5 cm). Turn the paper over and fold the bottom edge of the paper up 1" (2.5 cm) again. Continue turning the paper over and folding until the top is reached. Pick up the paper and pinch the bottom. Allow the top to fan out.

# Games *(cont.)*

## Materials:

- rubber ball (1 per 3 children)

## Monkey in the Middle

One student is chosen to be the "monkey." He or she stands in the middle of two players who are standing approximately 10' (3 m) apart, facing each other. The two players throw the ball to each other while the monkey tries to intercept the ball. The last player to touch the ball becomes the new monkey.

# Obstacle Courses

## Materials:

- varies according to the objects available and the location of the course (suggestions: natural obstacles, tires, jump ropes, boxes, etc.)

## Obstacle Course

Create your own obstacle course with objects that are available. The obstacles can be as easy or as complicated as you wish to make them. If you are using a playground, utilize the equipment already available, such as the swings, tunnels, and monkey bars. Or, obstacles can be created. For example, a jump rope can be tied low between two trees as a hurdle, or used for jumping a certain number of times. Use your imagination and creativity when setting up the course. Before beginning, demonstrate the course by walking through it a few times for the students so that they know what is expected at each station.

Create your own obstacle course by using the activity suggestions listed on page 228. Suggestions for obstacle courses requiring specific equipment are on pages 229–233.

There are a variety of ways of participating in obstacle courses. Try some of the suggestions below:

- Each student can proceed through the obstacle course for fun. Time is not kept. He or she simply practices each activity.

- The student can progress through the obstacle course alone. Time him or her. The student with the fastest time is the winner.

- Each team can progress through the obstacle course together. The team cannot proceed to the next activity until each member has completed the current activity. After being timed, the team with the fastest time is the winner.

- Spread the students out throughout the obstacle course. Each student does the activity at a station until a whistle is blown. Then, the student rotates to the next activity.

# Obstacle Courses *(cont.)*

## Create Your Own Obstacle Course

Creating your own obstacle course is easy and fun. All you have to do is sequence about 5–8 activities together. Below are some simple suggestions for making your own obstacle course; however, almost any of the activities in this book will work.

- animal walk (See pages 101–102.)
- bat an object (ball, balloon, beanbag, etc.)
- blow an object with a drinking straw
- blow bubbles
- bounce a ball
- bounce on a ball
- carry an object on a spoon
- clap
- crawl
- crawl over an object
- crawl under an object
- do a puzzle
- draw a picture
- fly like an airplane
- gallop
- hopscotch
- jump
- jump around an object
- jump rope

- jumping jacks
- kick a ball
- leap
- move an object from one place to another
- put a beanbag between knees and jump
- put on clothing
- ride a tricycle
- roll
- roll a ball
- run
- skip
- slide
- throw an object (ball, balloon, beanbag)
- toss a beanbag at a target
- use a broom to sweep a ball around cones
- walk backward
- walk forward
- wheelbarrow walk
- whirl around

# Obstacle Courses *(cont.)*

## Materials:

- rubber balls (2 different colors that fit inside coffee cans)
- boards and bricks to create ramps
- cardboard boxes, rocks, and other objects to create obstacles
- coffee cans (3 or more, opened on both ends and taped together to form tunnels)
- chalk, masking tape, or pebbles
- scissors

## Obstacle Course Kickball

Determine the start and finish lines, and mark them with chalk, tape, or pebbles. As a group, work together to create an obstacle course, including ramps, tunnels, cutouts from cardboard, chairs, etc., which the players will kick the balls through. Divide the players into teams of no fewer than two and no more than six players each. Explain the rules of the course, and choose someone to act as a referee. At the referee's signal, the first kicker on each team kicks the ball as far as possible along the course. The team member runs after his or her ball, kicking it along, and making sure to keep the ball as close to the route as possible. No team member may kick the ball more than twice in a row. The team member may not kick his or her opponent's ball away from the course. The first team to kick the ball across the finish line wins the game.

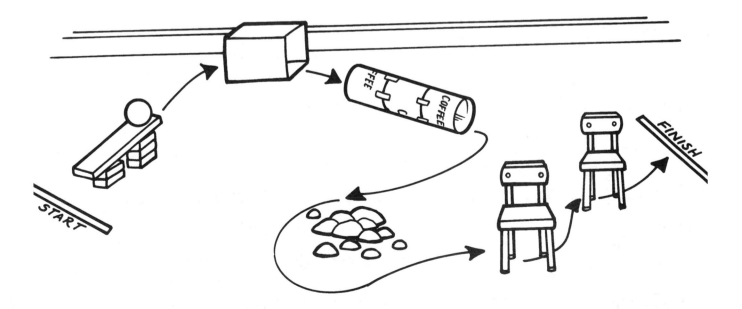

# Obstacle Courses *(cont.)*

## Materials:

- 24" (61 cm) piece of rope (1 per team)
- rubber ball (1 per team)
- wading pool
- toy boat (1 per team)
- balance beam or masking tape
- tricycle (1 per team)
- gunny sack (1 per team)

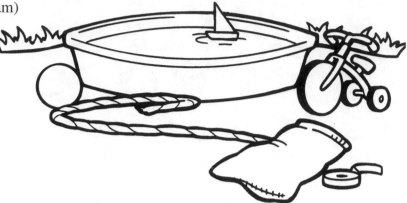

## Friendship Obstacle Course

To complete the Friendship Obstacle Course, divide the class into teams of two. Each team must complete the obstacle course together with friends.

The activities are listed below. Follow the diagram on page 231 for set up. Enlist adult help to stand as monitors throughout the course area.

---

**Activity 1—Three-Legged Run**
Teammates link bodies together by placing arms over each others' shoulders, and tie the two center legs together, and run around 3 cones.

**Activity 2—Throw a Ball-a-Thon**
The team tosses balls into the air 20 times while counting.

**Activity 3—Sailboat Race**
The team blows small boats across a wading pool.

**Activity 4—Crazy Walk**
The team walks on a balance beam, or tape line, backward!

**Activity 5—Cycle Fun**
The team rides big-wheel tricycles on a circular or linear course.

**Activity 6—Gunny Sack Race**
Team members get into the same sack and hop as quickly as possible to the finish line! Make sure the surface they hop over is soft.

---

**Safety Notes:** An adult must be posted at any activity involving water. It is possible for a child to drown in even 1" (2.5 cm) of water, so the greatest caution should be taken for a safe, pleasurable experience.

---

# Obstacle Courses (cont.)

## Friendship Obstacle Course (cont.)

**Activity 6—Gunny Sack Race**

**Activity 1—Three-Legged Run**

**Activity 5—Cycle Fun**

**Activity 2—Throw a Ball-a-Thon**

**Activity 4—Crazy Walk**

**Activity 3—Sailboat Race**

# Obstacle Courses (cont.)

## Materials:

- 2 benches
- 2 rubber balls or beach balls
- 4 cones
- 2 mats
- 4 hula hoops
- 3 umbrellas

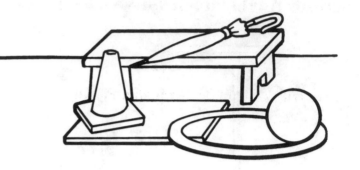

## Thematic Obstacles

Consider setting up an obstacle course to match a theme that you are currently teaching. The obstacle course below was created around a weather theme.

## Weather the Obstacles

Set up an obstacle course in the gym, or on the playground, as shown on page 233. Spread the children around the course. They may start anywhere, but need to complete each activity.

**Activity 1—Paddle Through a Flood**
    Sit on a bench. Move to the end by scooting along the bench.

**Activity 2—Don't Get a Sunburn!**
    Crawl under the umbrellas.

**Activity 3—Toss the Hailstone**
    Toss the ball in the air and catch it 10 times.

**Activity 4—Sail Between Islands in a Hurricane**
    Run around the cones, weaving in and out through them.

**Activity 5—Slide on the Ice**
    Lie down on the bench with tummy on the bench. Move to the end by scooting along the bench.

**Activity 6—Roll Down the Hill in Snow**
    Roll on a mat.

**Activity 7—Make Snow Angels**
    Lay on your back on the mat. Move your arms and legs.

**Activity 8—Jump over Puddles**
    Jump over hoops.

# Obstacle Courses *(cont.)*

## Weather the Obstacles *(cont.)*

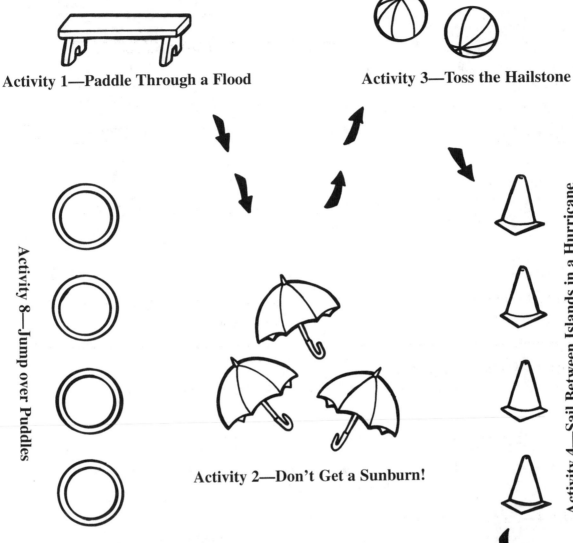

**Activity 1—Paddle Through a Flood**

**Activity 3—Toss the Hailstone**

**Activity 8—Jump over Puddles**

**Activity 4—Sail Between Islands in a Hurricane**

**Activity 2—Don't Get a Sunburn!**

**Activity 7—Make Snow Angels**

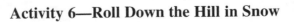

**Activity 5—Slide on the Ice**

**Activity 6—Roll Down the Hill in Snow**

# Relays

## Materials:

- 2 balloons
- 4 sets of chopsticks
- 2 cones

## Chopstick-Balloon Relay

Divide the players into teams, and line them up single file. Place a cone across from each line. Give sets of chopsticks to the first two people of each team. The first player of each team holds a balloon between his or her chopsticks. At the starting signal, the first player walks around the cone and returns to hand off the balloon to the second player, using only the chopsticks. The first player then gives the chopsticks to the third player while the second player runs off to make a lap around the cone. If a balloon is dropped, it can only be picked up by using the chopsticks. The play continues until every player has had the opportunity to make a lap around the cone. The first team to get all of its players back to the line is the winner.

## Materials:

- none

## Crab Relay

In this relay race, the runners crawl backward on all fours, "crab style," beginning at the starting line. When a player reaches the finish line, he or she runs back to the starting line and tags the next "crab," who repeats the action. The first team to have all of its players return to the starting line wins.

# Relays *(cont.)*

## Materials:

- 8–10 cones

## Caterpillar Relay

Divide the class into two teams. Direct the children to stand one behind the other in their respective teams. Have each child put his or her hands on the shoulders of the person in front of him or her. At the starting signal, children move as quickly as they can (continuing to hold on caterpillar-style), zig-zagging around the cones set up on the racing path. To complete the race, the teams must travel around the cone at the opposite end of the starting point and move back to the starting line. The first team back wins.

## Materials:

- small potato (1 per child)
- plastic spoons

## Potato Relay

Divide the players into two equal teams. Have each team form a line behind the starting line. Place a pile of potatoes, one for each player, at a line opposite the starting line. Give the first runner in each line a plastic spoon. At the starting signal, the players with the spoons must each run to the pile of potatoes and pick up one with the spoon. The player must balance the potato on the spoon, and walk or run back to the starting line. The players may not use his or her fingers to pick up or carry the potato. After dropping off the potato, the player then passes his or her spoon to the next player in the line. This continues until one of the teams returns all of its potatoes to the starting line and is declared the winner.

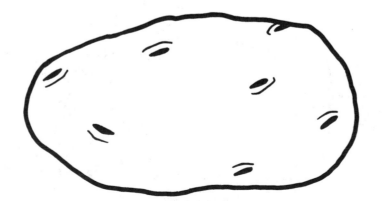

# Relays *(cont.)*

## Materials:

- a suitcase or shopping bag (1 per team)
- clothing (old pajamas, shirts, socks, etc.)

## Suitcase Relay

Before playing, pack each suitcase or bag with an equal number of clothing items (2–3). It is important to keep the items similar as well. Be sure the clothing is large enough to fit over the clothes of each player. Form two or more teams of equal size. Divide the teams in half, and have one group from each team line up at the starting line with the other group at the finish line approximately 20–30 yards (18–27 m) away. To begin, have the first player of each team open the suitcase and put on all of the items inside of it. Next, he or she carries the empty suitcase to the other side and removes the clothing, which the waiting player packs back into the suitcase. Then, the waiting player takes the suitcase and runs back to the starting line. This continues until each player has had a chance to be both the person who puts on the clothes and the person who packs the suitcase. The first team to have all of its players finish both tasks wins.

## Materials:

- 2 beanbags
- chalk

## Carry and Fetch Relay

Divide the players into two teams, and have each team form a line. Draw a chalk circle on the ground in front of each line. Give the first player in each team a beanbag. Upon the signal, the first player of each team carries the beanbag and places it inside the team circle. He or she then runs back and tags the hand of the second player who runs to the circle, retrieves the beanbag, and runs back to the line to hand it off to the third player. This pattern continues until all of the players on a team have made the run and are in their original positions. The first team to do so is declared the winner.

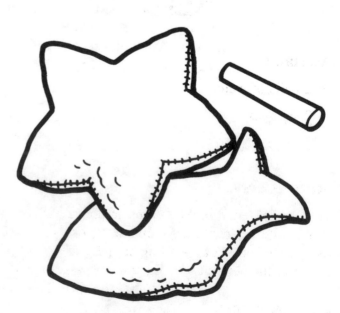

# Relays *(cont.)*

## Choo-Choo Relay

Divide the players into two lines, and have each player pick a partner from within the line. When the pair moves in this relay, it moves together as two "cars" of a train. One child stands behind the other and holds onto his or her partner's hips. Then the pair shuffles along without lifting the feet. At the signal to start, the first pair from each team goes to a designated turning point about 25' (7.6 m) away, switches positions, and heads back to the starting line where it tags the next pair who does the same thing. The first team to have all of its pairs complete the activity wins.

## Materials:

- 2 pails of water
- 2 sponges
- 2 large cups

## Water Relay

Divide the players into two teams and have each team form a line. Place a pail of water at the end of each line and an empty, large cup at the other end of the line. Give sponges to the players next to the pails. At the sound of a starting signal, each player with a sponge dips the sponge in the water and passes it to the next player. Each team passes the sponge from one player to the next until it reaches the last player who squeezes it into the cup. This continues until one team has filled its cup and is declared the winner.

# Play Dough Recipes

## Cooked Dough

### Ingredients:

4 cups (950 mL) flour

4 cups (950 mL) water

2 cups (475 mL) salt

2 tablespoons (30 mL) cooking oil

1 small container cream of tartar

food coloring

### Directions

Mix and heat until ingredients form a ball. Remove from heat when play dough reaches the correct consistency. Cool. Store in a sealed, air-tight container.

## No-Cook Dough

### Ingredients

2 cups (475 mL) self-rising flour

2 tablespoons (30 mL) alum

2 tablespoons (30 mL) cooking oil

2 tablespoons (30 mL) salt

1¼ cups (300 mL) boiling water

food coloring (optional)

### Directions

Mix and knead, adding food coloring if desired. Store in a sealed, air-tight container.

**Teacher Note:** To make Smelly Play Dough, follow the recipe above and add liquid flavorings for smell.

# Play Dough Recipes *(cont.)*

## No-Fail Dough

### Ingredients:

1½ cups (360 mL) flour

¼ cup (60 mL) salt

1½ cups (360 mL) water

1½ tablespoons (22 mL) cooking oil

food coloring (optional)

### Directions

Sift dry ingredients. Mix liquids and add coloring if desired. Pour dry ingredients into liquid mixture. Cook over low to moderate heat, stirring constantly, until thickened mixture begins to loosen from sides of the pan. Knead. Cool. Store in a plastic bag or air-tight container. (This dough does not need refrigeration.)

## Preschool Dough

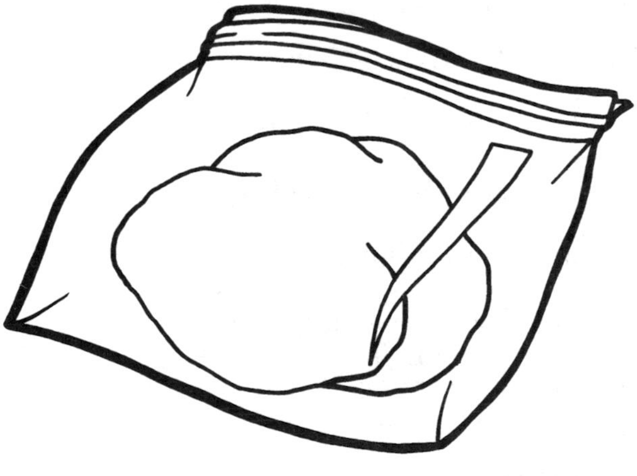

### Ingredients

2 cups (480 mL) flour

2 cups (480 mL) water

1 tablespoon (15 mL) oil

1 cup (240 mL) salt

2 teaspoons (10 mL) cream of tartar

food coloring (optional)

### Directions

Mix all ingredients together in a saucepan. Cook and stir until mixture thickens and starts to stick to the pan. Knead out the lumps. Cool completely. Store tightly covered.

# Paint Recipes

## Salt Paint

### Ingredients:

$\frac{1}{8}$ cup (30 mL) liquid starch

2 drops of food coloring

paper plates

$\frac{1}{8}$ cup (30 mL) water

$\frac{1}{2}$ cup (120 mL) salt

paintbrush

### Directions

Mix starch, water, food coloring, and salt. Use the paint with a paintbrush. Keep stirring the mixture while you use it. As the paint dries, it will crystallize.

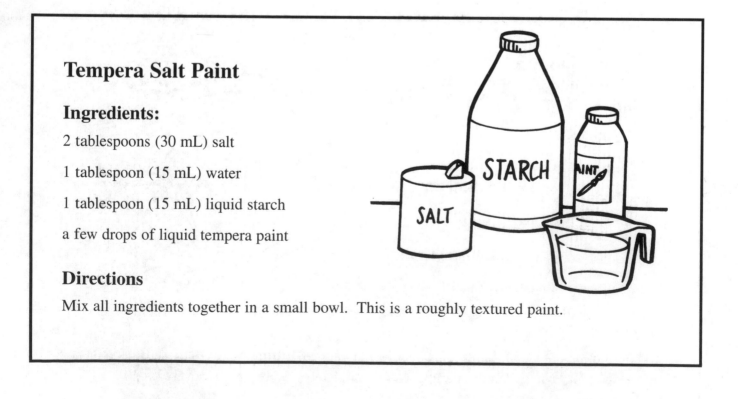

## Tempera Salt Paint

### Ingredients:

2 tablespoons (30 mL) salt

1 tablespoon (15 mL) water

1 tablespoon (15 mL) liquid starch

a few drops of liquid tempera paint

### Directions

Mix all ingredients together in a small bowl. This is a roughly textured paint.